January Bible Study

1 PETER:
MESSAGE OF
ENCOURAGEMENT

John H. McClanahan

Convention Press • Nashville, Tennessee

Dedicated
to
Jim Fowler and Hazel Loe McClanahan
Godly Parents
Who by
Precept and Example
Brought Me up
in the
Nurture and Admonition of the Lord

Contents

This book is the text for a course in the subject area Bible Study of the Church Study Course.

Target group: This book is designed for adults and is part of the Church Study Course offerings. The 1963 statement of "The Baptist Faith and Message" is the doctrinal guideline for the writer and editor.

Dewey Decimal Classification Number: 227.92
Subject Heading: Bible N. T. 1 Peter
Printed in the United States of America.

A Word to Begin

From Rome, Peter wrote to Christians living in Asia Minor. These believers were undergoing some degree of opposition and threat. His letter for tough times was meant to inspire, instruct, exhort, and encourage his Christian friends. Their trials would test the metal of their faith and prove it to be genuine; such open proof would issue in praise, honor, and glory at Christ's return. They could face the pressures and dangers of their situation in the confident knowledge of a future inheritance kept in heaven for them. As pilgrims and exiles in their world, they were to live in a superlative manner; they were to live as God's servants in creative and responsible freedom, imitating Christ and sharing his sufferings.

John H. McClanahan, pastor of First Baptist Church, Pine Bluff, Arkansas, is the author of this textbook. You may use it in personal or group study. In both uses, the Personal Learning Activities at the end of each chapter will help the learner to review the material covered. In group study, the companion Study Guide will provide helpful resources for the teacher and the members. The Teaching Guide will aid the teacher in directing the study. In this textbook, guidance for using Personal Learning Activities is in the section entitled "The Church Study Course" at the end of the book.

Also at the back of the book is a Church Study Course Credit request (Form 151). On completion of this book, the pupil should mail in the completed form to the address indicated. Two copies of the credit award will be mailed to the applicant's church—one for the church's record, the other for the pupil's.

ELI LANDRUM, JR., editor

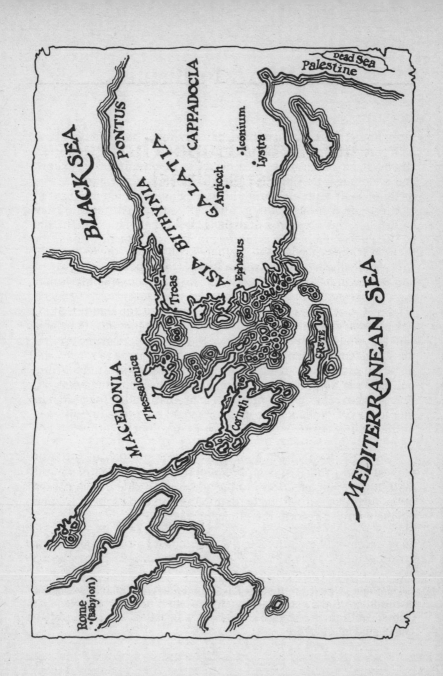

1

Our Living Hope Through Jesus Christ

1 Peter 1:1-12

It grew harder and harder. Even within these four walls there was too much misery, too much seemingly pointless suffering. Every day something else failed to make sense, something else grew too heavy. . . .

But as the rest of the world grew stranger, one thing became increasingly clear . . . our Bible was the center of an ever-widening circle of help and hope. Like waifs clustered around a blazing fire, we gathered about it, holding out our hearts to its warmth and light. . . . Life in Ravensbruck took place on two separate levels, mutually impossible. One, the observable, external life, grew every day more horrible. The other, the life we lived with God, grew daily better, truth upon truth, glory upon glory.[1]

George K. Schweitzer, a distinguished scientist and dedicated Christian, related an intriguing personal incident which occurred in Louisville, Kentucky, a few years ago. He was in the Blue Grass State to deliver a series of lectures at the University of Louisville. Louisville was having an extremely cold January that year. Early one morning, Dr. Schweitzer was standing on a street corner waiting for a bus. A stiff wind was whistling around him. His first lecture was scheduled for 9:00 AM. He was giving himself a bit more than an hour to catch the bus and arrive at the university campus on time. Although he was dressed for the season, as he stood waiting for the bus he became increasingly aware of just how cold the morning really was.

As Dr. Schweitzer stood waiting for his bus, he became aware of another person standing nearby, just under the awning of a rather dilapidated old store building. This person, a little old lady, also appeared to be cold. Dr. Schweitzer guessed that she was about seventy years old. She wore a coat, but it was old and tattered. As he became colder, he knew that she must be colder still. Thinking of the hot breakfast which he had enjoyed a short time ago, he wondered if the little old lady had eaten anything that morning.

Finally, Dr. Schweitzer was unable to stand by and do nothing in the face of such need. He walked over to the little old lady and slipped a dollar into her coat pocket. His bus was arriving. He said to her, "Chin up!" and boarded his bus.

On the following morning, Dr. Schweitzer was standing on the same street corner. Suddenly, the little old lady appeared again in what seemed like a replay of the previous morning. But this time, the woman approached the guest scientist. His first thought was prompted by dismay: "Oh, no! I've started something. She'll be here every morning this week expecting a dollar!" No sooner had he made this judgment, however, than she reached out to slip a twenty-dollar bill into his hand. With the faint trace of a smile, she said: "Congratulations, buddy. 'Chin Up' paid twenty to one!"[2]

In sharp contrast to the subtle humor of this situation, 1 Peter is a straightforward message of genuine encouragement which carries no element of deceit or surprise. A "Chin up!" mood pervades the book, which includes declaration and exhortation (5:12). The declaration affirmed what "the true grace of God" (5:12) through Jesus Christ had done for those persons who believed. The exhortation urged the new converts to stand fast in their faith.

Salutation (1:1-2)

Authorship (1:1)

The salutation of 1 Peter clearly identifies the author as "Peter, an apostle of Jesus Christ" (v. 1). In our day, we are accustomed to finding the writer's name at the close of a letter. How many times have you started to read a letter by looking first at the signature to see who had written you!

The accepted style of first-century correspondence, however, placed the sender's name in the salutation or at the beginning of a letter. This pattern was reflected clearly in Paul's New Testament letters (Rom. 1:1; 1 Cor. 1:1; Gal. 1:1; Phil. 1:1). That same style occurred in other letters from this era which have been discovered in historical research and/or archaeological digs.

The specific person identified by the salutation in 1 Peter is the Simon Peter whom we know in the Gospels as the Galilean fisherman. He became the recognized leader among Jesus' twelve disciples. Across the years, the possibility of another author has been explored and, at times, advocated. The letter's internal evidence, however, affirms Peter's authorship. The external evidence from early church writers also confirms Peter's authorship. For our study, we will accept Peter's authorship with confidence and integrity.

Peter made use of an amanuensis, or secretary, in writing his letter. In the closing postscript, he declared: "By Silvanus, a faithful brother as I regard him, I have written briefly to you" (5:12). We believe that this person was Silas, the Greek Christian who traveled with Paul on the second missionary journey (Acts 15:40 to 18:22). He was associated with Paul when Paul wrote the two letters to the Thessalonian Christians (1 Thess. 1:1; 2 Thess. 1:1). In the Thessalonian letters as well as in 1 Peter, the name was spelled "Silvanus."

In the Greek language, the expression **by Silvanus** (1 Pet. 5:12) means *through Silvanus*. Peter and his secretary probably were following a well-established first-century practice for preparing letter manuscripts. A competent scribe could be given a free hand in writing the final copy of any dictation. In terms of style and language, 1 Peter ranks with Hebrews as being the best literary writing in the New Testament. Thus, Silvanus must have been an able scribe. The thought and content of 1 Peter, however, remained that of Simon Peter.

We should note the title which Peter openly declared for himself—"an apostle of Jesus Christ" (v. 1). The word **apostle** literally means *one sent forth* as a messenger. In the early church, the word tended to be limited to those who were eyewitnesses to Jesus' life and ministry, those whom he commissioned to carry his message throughout the world. (The term was not an exclusive word for the twelve. In Acts 14:4,14, the title was given to Barnabas. In Romans 16:7, the title possibly was given to Andronicus and Junias.) Paul considered himself to be an eyewitness because of his vital, personal encounter with the risen Christ on the Damascus road. Thus he, too, was an "apostle" (1 Cor. 15:7-9). Peter was one of Jesus' companions who participated in his ministry. But Christ commissioned both men to be his authoritative spokesmen.

Time and Place Setting (1:1-2)

First Peter was addressed specifically "to the exiles of the Dispersion" (v. 1). Those exiles lived in five well-known provinces which in the first century made up the bulk of Asia Minor. Both words, exiles and Dispersion, had a rich heritage in Judaism. The Hebrews had been displaced Exiles in Egypt and Babylon during the Old Testament era. During the New Testament period, the term "Dispersion," or diaspora in the Greek, often was used to refer to all Jewish people who were not living on the Palestinian mainland. The words "exiles" and "Dispersion" in the salutation of 1 Peter have caused some New Testament students to conclude that 1 Peter was addressed primarily to Jewish Christians.

On the other hand, considerable internal evidence in 1 Peter seems to reflect a Gentile group as recipients of the letter. For example, the statement, "Once you were no people but now you are God's people" (2:10), recalls Paul's use of these words from Hosea to describe Gentiles who had become Christians (Rom. 9:25-26; 11:30-31). Again, the statement, "You know that you were ransomed from the futile ways inherited from your fathers" (1 Peter 1:18), reads more like a description of former pagans than of former Jews. The term "futile" was used consistently in the Old Testament for idol worship; this indicates a stronger Gentile than Jewish rootage.

As we examine other related passages which appear throughout 1 Peter, we will note evidence of a mixed audience. Moreover, when we remember that other first-century churches were composed of both Jewish and Gentile people, we may conclude safely that 1 Peter likely was addressed to mixed congregations. These congregations included both Jews and Gentiles. If a majority group were to be named, most likely these churches were predominantly Gentile.

The Gentile-Jewish congregations which Peter addressed were located in five provinces of first-century Asia Minor: Pontus, Galatia, Cappadocia, Asia, and Bithynia (v. 1). This land area comprises a major part of modern Turkey.

Pontus was a northern coastal province on the Black Sea. The rugged Pontus mountains made inland travel difficult in this area, but the Black Sea was an open avenue leading through the Sea of Marmara and the Hellespontus (which we call the Dardanelles) to the Aegean and the Mediterranean Seas. Residents in Pontus had become a great maritime people.

Galatia originally was named for the Celtic invaders who came east from France, or Gaul. They were known as "Galli," hence as Galatians. This province formed the central land area of Asia Minor. It is best known by Christians from Paul's Letter to the Galatians in the New Testament.

Cappadocia was on the eastern limits of these five provinces. We might compare this area to the great expanses of land to the west during the settling of the continental United States. Cappadocia was a type of frontier land. It was a wild, mountainous country with few large cities. A developed highway ran from Tarsus near the southern coastline of Asia Minor north through Cappadocia to Pontus.

Asia, the westernmost of the five provinces, was regarded as the richest. In fact, it was considered to be one of the most highly developed provinces in the entire Roman Empire. Primary sources of wealth were agriculture, minerals, and timber. The province possessed a high degree of culture and intellectual activity. Not one but several chief cities were located in the Roman province of Asia: Ephesus, Smyrna, Sardis, and Pergamum. Emperor worship became popular and powerful in the province of Asia during the peace and prosperity inaugurated by Augustus Caesar.

Bithynia was located north and east from the Roman province of Asia, but south of Pontus. Like Pontus, Bithynia had some northern coastline on the Black Sea. In fact, the two areas often were organized into a single province. One of our best sources of information about conditions in this district is the Letters of Pliny the Younger, a Roman Commissioner for Bithynia-Pontus in AD 111-13. In his day, the number of Christians in Bithynia was high. Pliny wrote to the Roman Emperor Trajan that Christianity had spread even to the villages and rural districts. This seems to imply that even the least Hellenized areas (areas affected by Greek culture) were reached by Christian evangelization.

From New Testament references, we know that Jews from Cappadocia, Pontus, and Asia were in Jerusalem on the Day of Pentecost (Acts 2:9). Some of these persons likely were among the three thousand people converted to Christ on that day (Acts 2:41). As

11

these individuals returned to their homes, they well may have been the first Christian witnesses in their respective lands. Also, we know that Paul's first two missionary journeys carried him into this area, particularly through Galatia and Asia. On the second journey, Paul was prevented from going into Bithynia by "the Spirit of Jesus" (Acts 16:7). Perhaps the gospel already was being proclaimed well there.

We have reconstructed the initial setting of 1 Peter: Simon Peter of Galilee, an apostle of Jesus Christ, wrote to Christians living in five provinces of Asia Minor. Today, we might ask: From where was the letter postmarked?

Probably, the answer to the question is the city of Rome. First Peter 5:13 includes the statement: "She who is at Babylon, who is likewise chosen, sends you greetings." In all probability, the location is not to be taken literally. Likely, Peter was not in the Mesopotamian Valley, the specific spot for Babylon, when he wrote his letter.

In the Book of Revelation, John used the image of the city of Babylon to refer to the city of Rome (Rev. 17:1,5,9,18; 18:1-2). We conclude that in his letter, Peter did the same thing. Thus, 1 Peter would be postmarked from Rome. With the general flow of missionary movement in the New Testament from Jerusalem to the north and west, we easily can think of Peter, Silvanus, and Mark (1 Pet. 5:13) being together in Rome. To say that "all roads lead to Rome" was more than just a casual saying in that time. By the same token, for us to imagine that these three persons were together in Babylon is difficult.

Locating the origin of Peter's letter in Rome also helps us to determine its approximate date. Peter's death likely occurred in the middle to later sixties (AD 64-67). Also, the historical record shows that the Roman Emperor Nero initiated the first large-scale persecution of Christians in Rome after a great fire swept through the city in AD 64.

Later historians wrote that Nero blamed the Christians for the fire. His reprisals against the Christians were devastating. How Peter could have counseled loyalty and honor to the Emperor (2:13-17) after Nero persecuted the Christians is difficult to comprehend. The spectre of persecution in 1 Peter was real, but as yet it appeared not to have been the official Roman policy when Peter wrote. Thus, though some scholars suggest other dates, I favor a date in the early sixties (AD 61-63) for the writing of 1 Peter.

Theme and Purpose (1:1-2)

The factor of persecution brings us again to the "Chin up!" mood which pervades all of 1 Peter. This triumphant mood has caused 1 Peter to be described as the Epistle of Courage, the Epistle of Pilgrimage, or the Epistle of Hope.

Interpreters have given 1 Peter lavish praise as one of the persecution documents from the New Testament. The letter was a strong affirmation of hope at a time when evil threatened to prevail. It merits a place in the world's great literature expressing the glory of Christian courage in coping with life's hardships.

As our study progresses, we will see again and again how much this letter is a declaration of Christian courage, Christian pilgrimage, and Christian hope. The courage which Peter affirmed is far more than the "grin-and-bear-it" endurance of the Stoics. His sense of pilgrimage had far more meaning than a fairy-tale search for the pot of gold at the end of a rainbow. And his sense of hope was much more than a nebulous sense of optimism which wished that somehow, things would turn out all right in the end.

The hope of 1 Peter ultimately is based not on people but on God. The author's thought came from the main stream of salvation-history in the Old and New Testaments. The great Creator-God also is the gracious Redeemer-God who has made himself known through mighty acts or events in history. The God who brought Israel out of Egypt in the miraculous Exodus is the same God who raised Jesus Christ from the dead. The living God has given the resurrected Christ an indestructible glory so that our faith and hope in him may be steadfast and sure. God has promised faithful Christian pilgrims an inheritance at the end of life's journey which is "imperishable, undefiled, and unfading" (1:4).

The recovery of such a way of hope may be one of the greatest needs of contemporary men and women. So many people today live fear-filled lives. They are frightened by the spectre of nuclear war and communist domination. Some are afraid of air pollution and the stealthy growth of cancer cells. Many fear growing older and losing their security and/or their independence.

In a real sense, no part of the human race ever has "had it so good" as this generation. So many of us, remembering where we started in life in comparison with where we now are, must honestly say: "We've come a long way!" Yet many of us tend to live in an atmosphere of chronic fear. If such a way of fear is a sign of our times—and many commentators would say that it is—then the highway of hope which runs through 1 Peter has a great message for each of us.

Salutation Concluded (1:2)
In addition to the many introductory matters which are implied in the salutation (v. 1), let us note the significant ideas which conclude the salutation. We seldom find so many great themes sounded in just one verse of Scripture.

Peter indicated that the Gentile-Jewish exiles of the Dispersion had been "chosen" and "destined" by God (v. 2). The word **chosen** often is translated *elect,* and the term **destined** literally means *foreknown.*

Paul often used the words *chosen* and *destined* together to refer to God's initiative in calling a people to himself for some special purpose (Rom. 8:29; Eph. 1:4-5). In the Old and the New Testaments, the biblical doctrine of election does not indicate some special merit on the part of the individual or group being called. Instead, the emphasis always is on God's unmerited favor. Furthermore, those elected by God were not called for greater status, but for greater service. As Israel had received God's electing grace in the Old Testament, Christians now are the New Israel, recipients of God's electing favor and call to service.

We should note that the term **destined** did not mean *predestined.* The Greek word literally meant *to know before,* or *foreknowledge.* The word carried no idea of previously determined behavior or response. Such manipulation was not considered in character for the way in which God related to mankind. This word will appear again in 1 Peter. Peter obviously did not feel that God's activity in choosing the Christian exiles in any way undercut their freedom of will or their freedom of choice.

Believers who have been called by God, the Father, to receive his electing love also have been "sanctified by the Spirit for obedience to Jesus Christ" (v. 2). Although Baptists generally do not use the word *sanctification* as much as some other church groups do, it is a good, authentic New Testament word. However, it does not refer to a second-blessing, sinless-perfection status for Christians. The root meaning of the verb **sanctify** is *to consecrate* or *to dedicate* in the sense of setting something apart for holy service to God. Sanctification in this manner could be experienced by all believers in Christ. Peter's wording indicated that to lead believers to new levels of dedication to God is a part of the work of the "Spirit," that is, the Holy Spirit.

All of the words in verse 2 are a part of the Old Testament covenant language whereby people were invited to enter a special relationship with the living God. When they were established, covenants were expressions of God's favor, the gift of his grace. But the gift also carried with it the idea of demand. Covenant people were expected to obey the demands of their unique relationship with God. Consequently, Peter was in the mainstream of covenant thought as he pointed to the Holy Spirit's work of fostering "obedience to Jesus Christ" (v. 2).

The name *Jesus Christ* became the fuller title by which the carpenter-teacher from Nazareth was known. **Jesus** is a Greek form of the Hebrew name **Joshua** which means *deliverer* or *savior*. **Christ** is a Greek term which translated the Hebrew title **Messiah** which meant *the anointed one*.

The reference to the "sprinkling of his [Christ's] blood" likely is a further example of the covenant language which runs through this passage. In the establishment of the covenant at Sinai, obedience and sprinkling of the blood were mentioned (Ex. 24:7-8). In the context of 1 Peter 1:2, Peter likely referred to the forgiving and cleansing effect of Christ's atoning death on the cross for all our sins.

Looking at verse 2 as a whole, you will see that reference is made to God the Father, the (Holy) Spirit, and Jesus Christ. Quite obviously, the wording here reflects a trinitarian view of God's total person. We do not find a fully developed, formal doctrine of the Trinity in the New Testament. Many references like the one in 1 Peter 1:2, however, indicate that the trinitarian idea was a part of New Testament thought.

Peter closed his salutation to his Christian friends with a prayer: "May grace and peace be multiplied to you" (v. 2). The words *grace* and *peace* have a familiar New Testament ring. They appear in 2 Peter 1:2. All of Paul's letters include these words as a part of the salutations. From such repetition, we may conclude that the early Christians used these terms rather widely to express a prayer of blessing or benediction. Linguistically, *grace* or *charis* primarily is a Greek concept. The word pictures God's unmerited favor as it works redemptively in believers' hearts. On the other hand, *peace (eirēnē)* or *shalom* primarily is a Hebrew idea. The word pictures the condition of the heart when God's grace has done its work. **Shalom** is far more than just a truce or armistice. More than a mere cessation of hostilities, **shalom** refers to the *state of mutual well-being* where positive forces of good can begin rebuilding in the wake of war's devastation. It is all that makes for a person's highest good under God's rule. In the familiar New Testament prayer form, the two words are always in the same order. In a real sense, we may say that grace must come first and do its work before peace can be in any person's heart.

An Affirmation of Hope (1:3-9)

A Doxology of Praise (1:3*a*)
Peter moved from the salutation of his letter to a doxology of praise, a prayer of thanksgiving: "Blessed be the God and Father of our Lord Jesus Christ!" (1:3). Notice that no shadow of doubt or uncertainty clouded Peter's approach to God. Note even the punctuation in the Revised Standard Version. The first sentence closed not with a question mark, but with an exclamation mark!

In the New Testament, the verbal adjective translated "blessed" is used only regarding God.

The real reason for Peter's praise, however, was not just his confidence in God's existence. The fact that God is, is great. But the greatest discovery is made in knowing what God has done. God the Father has made himself fully known in his Son, Jesus Christ. Simon Peter would have liked the following lines from one of Fanny Crosby's hymns:

> To God be the glory, great things He hath done;
> So loved He the world that He gave us His Son.

A Living Hope (1:3*b*)
Peter sounded a trumpet note which is the resounding refrain of his entire letter for all Christians: "We have . . . a living hope through . . . Jesus Christ" (v. 3). His language is rich with vivid imagery and perceptive theological understanding.

Christian hope is the virtue of those persons who keep on believing that God's ways ultimately will be vindicated in people when they keep on praying,

> Thy kingdom come,
> Thy will be done,
> On earth as it is in heaven.
> Matthew 6:10

Hope, as such, is the opposite of despair. A **living hope** is *hope which refuses to give up and die.* Peter's hope was not illusion or fantasy. It was based on his confidence in God's moral character and on his belief in Christ's resurrection.

Peter declared that the Christian's living hope through Christ begins with a new spiritual birth. Reminiscent of Jesus' conversation with Nicodemus, Peter wrote of Christians as persons who had been born again, or born anew (v. 3).

Individuals are offered the opportunity to experience the new birth because of God's "mercy" (v. 3). We are born again not because of our merit, but because of God's mercy extended toward us. This thought is similar to Paul's idea of God's grace as his unmerited favor bestowed on us.

The key to the entire matter of being born again and knowing a "living hope" is found in Jesus' resurrection from the dead (v. 3). No other experience in Jesus' life and ministry can assume greater importance than his resurrection. Peter would agree with John's emphasis in the Fourth Gospel that the resurrection is the greatest of all Jesus' miracles or signs. Indeed, the two would agree that the miraculous power demonstrated in the resurrection validated all of Jesus' previous signs.

By the resurrection of Christ, God had kindled a hope in Christians that could not be extinguished. In fact, real doubt exists that the Christian movement ever would have come into being apart from the resurrection. The early Christians' conviction that Jesus was alive again after his crucifixion and burial transformed a band of weak disciples into a missionary force which carried the gospel throughout the Greco-Roman world. First and foremost, the Christian faith is a resurrection faith.

In old Judaism, the Pharisees had hoped for a resurrection after death. The Greek philosophers had written seriously about the possibility of the soul's immortality. For Christians, however, Jesus' resurrection changed a hopeless dread—or, at best, uncertainty—into a living hope. This mighty act of God gave their hope proof and permanence.

An Eternal Inheritance (1:4-5)
Although Peter did not use the word *family*, his next metaphor had a definite family connotation. Christians not only have been born again to a living hope, they also have been born anew "to an inheritance which is imperishable, undefiled, and unfading"

(v. 4). Peter indicated to his readers that God had received them into his family. Again, this reflects a thought which we also find in Paul's letters (Eph. 2:19). The word translated "inheritance" (1 Pet. 1:4) was an accepted Greek term which referred to property received by an heir, usually someone in a direct family line.

An Enduring Inheritance (1:4)—Peter used three adjectives to describe Christians' inheritance. All three words point to the permanent, enduring nature of the inheritance. The term **imperishable** means *not subject to decay or spoiling.* The word **undefiled** means *pure or unstained by filth* in a spiritual or moral sense. The term **unfading** means *unwithering;* cut flowers are doomed to wither and die, but flowers growing in fertile soil will not wither or fade.

The word **unwithering** (*amaranton*) has an athletic connotation. Greek and Roman athletes competed in the various sports events to win garland crowns made of ivy, flowers, or celery leaves. The expenditure of time and energy to win these crowns was mammoth, yet the crowns that the victors won soon withered. In contrast to such short-lived reward, pilgrim victors in the Christian race of life would receive a crown which would last forever.

A further comment should be made about the three descriptive adjectives in verse 4. We do not see this in the English translation, but in the Greek all three of these words begin with the letter *a*: *aphtharton, amianton,* and *amaranton.* Thus, a bit of alliteration is an integral part of this verse. This fact plus other matters of style and language which we will note as we move along have made some students think that Peter may have composed his letter from various sermonic materials.

Additional rich symbolism is a part of two of these Greek adjectives. The term *amiantos* referred to a mineral which was found in certain rock formations of the Greco-Roman world. A process had been discovered whereby fabrics treated with this mineral became fire-resistant. Though soiled, a fabric so treated would turn pure white when placed in the fire. Romans would pay generously for this mineral, because they used it to prepare their dead for burial. In the cremation process that the Romans often used, *amiantos* preserved the precious ashes in a fabric unaffected by the fire. Thus, Peter indicated that the Christian inheritance is free from all taint of defilement. When placed under

18

pressure, it becomes even more pure. It will stand, even in the fiery judgment.

The word *amarantos*, without the alpha privative which is like the prefix *un* or *non* in English, was the name of a flower known in the ancient world: the maranth. This flower or plant gave the appearance of being dead; yet it was alive and enduring. Peter picked up this word to declare that the Christian inheritance is not subject to the ordinary laws of transiency. It will endure, even when adverse circumstances make it appear to be dead.

Peter added a further thought about Christians' "inheritance." It is a legacy which is "kept in heaven for [believers], who by God's power are guarded through faith for a salvation ready to be revealed in the last time" (vv. 4-5). The term "kept" also is translated "reserved" (v. 4, KJV).

Contemporary people who travel a great deal are aware of the importance of advance reservations. Traveling salespersons know the value of a dependable reservation system for insuring them a place to stay each evening. Families planning vacations often make reservations months in advance, especially if they are going to some resort area. Many of us also know the frustration which comes when a reservation did not hold.

At the risk of sounding a bit casual, we may say that in verse 4 Peter declared: Christians have reservations made in heaven which will not be canceled under any circumstances. The verb "kept" or "reserved" is in the perfect tense in Greek; the perfect tense refers to action which already has taken place in the past, still continues, and will continue to hold good in the future.

Of necessity, our generation has become extremely security conscious. Because of the increase in home and business break-ins, many of us have devised rather elaborate deterrent systems in an effort to insure adequate protection from an outside intruder and/or thief. Even with our careful forethought, however, some of us wonder how safe our valuables really are.

An Assured Inheritance (1:5).—Against the backdrop of our generally fearful insecurity, we should note Peter's affirmation that God's power guards Christians' inheritance (v. 5). The picture is of God's being like a mighty fortress, as Martin Luther wrote in his great Reformation hymn. The believers' inheritance is garrisoned in this impregnable stronghold. Can you imagine any greater security system than this?

Peter declared that faith commits a person to God's keeping power. Not human prowess but God's presence, like a watchman at the door of the stronghold, guards the security of those who trust in him. Peter's thought at this point affirms our Baptist belief in the eternal security of the believer.

As defined by Peter, the ultimate goal of God's care is "for a salvation ready to be revealed in the last time" (v. 5). The word *salvation* is used in the New Testament in several different ways. Most often, the word appears in one of three ways. I like to refer to this usage as the three dimensions of salvation.

For example, the word *salvation* may refer to the initial experience of coming to know the Savior. Jesus said to Zacchaeus: " 'Today salvation has come to this house' " (Luke 19:9). Again, the term *salvation* may refer to a process whereby a person cooperates with God to work a possession into a finished product. Paul wrote his dear friends in Philippi: "Work out your own salvation with fear and trembling" (Phil. 2:12). Or, the same word may refer to the final victory and consummation of God's work of redemption at the end of time and Christ's second coming (Rom. 13:11; Heb. 9:28). The word occurs in 1 Peter 1:5 in the latter sense. We will see the full and complete revelation of God's salvation only at the end, "in the last time" (v. 5). For most of us, this will be at the time of our deaths. For the entire human race, it will be at the end of the age and Christ's return.

Tried by Fire (1:6-7)

Peter's belief in a future heavenly home for all faithful Christians was vividly real. However, this did not cause him to be primarily futuristic in his faith. His religion was not just "pie-in-the-sky, by-and-by, when-you-die." He believed that the Christian faith had strong here-and-now dimensions. He referred to this important area of life and work in verse 6. Christians truly may "rejoice" (v. 6) because of their secure inheritance with God which will be made known at the end. Also, they must be ready to cope with the difficult, demanding issues of life as they are being lived out in any day.

Peter's turning to matters at hand for his readers introduced the persecution theme in his letter: "though now for a little while you may have to suffer various trials" (v. 6). We should note that Peter wrote: You *may* have to suffer. Some of what the Christians feared evidently had not happened. No doubt, some harshness and reprisals had occurred. The ominous clouds were gathering, but the storm's full fury had not broken.

From later sources outside the biblical literature, we know that outright, direct persecution came to Christians living in the immediate area to which 1 Peter was addressed. For example, a letter from Pliny, the governor of Bithynia, written to the Roman Emperor Trajan in AD 110, contained this section about the official policy against Christians: " 'With those who have been bought before me as Christians, I have pursued the following course: I have asked them if they were Christians, and if they have confessed, I have asked them a second and a third time, threatening them with punishment: if they have persisted, I have commanded them to be led away to punishment.' "[3]

The actual situation that Peter addressed, however, likely was much earlier than this. We have dated his letter in the early 60's before Nero unleashed the initial bloodbath vendetta against Christians in AD 64. At that time, the persecution probably was not sanctioned by the government. It may have stemmed from opposition groups who were trying to enlist government approval for what they were doing. This would make the persecution more like organized opposition and violent measures that did not have full government endorsement.

To encourage his readers to set their sails to cope with the strong persecution winds, Peter used a metaphor from the process of smelting. Metals were refined—made more pure—by fire. Peter reminded his friends that even a precious metal like gold could be refined and made more valuable by fire (v. 7). He concluded that for Christians, persecution should be like fire for gold. The genuineness of their faith should become more evident as they endured hard times.

The word translated "genuineness" was a term from the money market of Peter's day. Genuine coins were the opposite of counterfeit coins. Peter stated that genuine faith which had passed through the fire would be more praiseworthy to God when Jesus Christ returns.

Faith's Outcome (1:8-9)

Mentioning Jesus' name seemed to remind Peter of the great devotion which his friends in the five provinces held for the Lord: "Without having seen him you love him" (v. 8). No eyewitnesses to Jesus' life and ministry were present in these groups. Peter's language seems to hint, however, that he was an eyewitness. As such, this line points to apostolic authorship which is added evidence that Simon Peter wrote 1 Peter.

The wording of verse 8 is similar to Jesus' statement to Thomas in one of the resurrection appearances recorded in the Fourth Gospel (John 20:29). A. T. Robertson pointed out the interesting possibility that Peter would have heard the conversation just as John did. Thus, he could have used the words before John wrote his Gospel.[4]

Peter concluded that the immediate end of a devotion to Christ which embraced both love and belief was "joy" (v. 8). This joy is beyond human words to express. The ultimate end of such devotion and faith is the salvation of believers' souls (v. 9). **Soul** is the New Testament word which refers to *the total person*.

An Announcement of Grace (1:10-12)

Peter closed the section 1:1-12 of his letter with a summary description of Jewish prophecy as being a triumphant announcement of God's grace made known in Christ. In essence, Peter declared that the longings of the old prophets found their fulfillment in Christ and the redemption he worked.

Peter concluded that the Old Testament prophets wrote of a grace which actually reached far beyond their generation. They searched and inquired diligently about the anticipated salvation (v. 10), but it did not become known in their day. They inquired about a person through whom, and a time when, God's redemption would come to pass (v. 11). They even predicted "the sufferings of Christ and the subsequent glory" (v. 11). These words may be an early Christian reference relating Jesus' life to Isaiah 53. Through all this, Peter obviously felt that prophecy had a *fore*-telling and a *forth*-telling dimension.

Peter identified the guiding light for the prophets as "the Spirit of Christ within them" (v. 11). Peter seemed to mean that the Old Testament prophets knew something of Jesus even though they did not call him by that name.

God revealed to the prophets that they were not serving themselves and their generation (v. 12). Their work pointed primarily to an age and a time in the future.

Now we come to Peter's clinching declaration. The age which

had been foretold and eagerly anticipated was the era of the specific generation which he was addressing. The people to whom Peter was writing were among the first generation to hear the triumphant announcement of God's grace which was made known through Christ. That which the prophets had longed to know and that of which angels longed to catch a glimpse (v. 12) now was the ready, available possession of those who believed in Christ!

The wisdom of great sages in the past was eclipsed by a simple child's knowledge of God's grace and truth through Christ. So we affirm that whether Christians lived in the first century or they live in the twentieth century, they had and have a living hope through Jesus Christ.

Lessons for Life from 1 Peter 1:1-12

God does not want his children to be cowered by a spirit of fear.—Of all people, Christians have the greatest reasons for living—even in the midst of difficulty—with a "chin-up" attitude. Such courageous life-styles are based on what God in Christ already has done for all persons who believe. The Christian hope is not just pie-in-the-sky, when-you-die. The Christian hope is "Emmanuel"—God with us!

Christian hope is the opposite of despair.—Too many people wander through life as though it were a maze, unsure that they ever will find any light at the end of the tunnel. By faith, Christians live life as a pilgrimage, confident that God will be vindicated in the family of humanity. Such a hope refuses to give up or die. Peter based his hope on God's moral character and on his belief in Jesus' resurrection. He wanted to share his authentic hope with his readers. That includes you!

Christians are the recipients of the grandest good news which ever has been told.—People's search for God has been realized in the revelation of Jesus Christ. The inquiries into the nature of truth and salvation have been fulfilled. That which the prophets had longed to know and the angels longed to see is the possession of all who believe in Christ. This was good news when Peter initially announced it to people living in the first century. It is equally good news for people who hear it for the first time in the twentieth century.

1. Corrie ten Boom, *The Hiding Place* (Carmel, N.Y.: Guideposts Associates, Inc., 1971), pp. 177-78.

2. George K. Schweitzer, "The Protestant Work Ethic," *Christians Confronting the Economic Crisis* (Nashville: SBC Christian Life Commission, 1974) p. 50.

3. Benjamin W. Robinson, *The Abingdon Bible Commentary* (New York: Abingdon Press, 1929), p. 1338.

4. A. T. Robertson, *Word Pictures in the New Testament* (Nashville: Broadman Press, 1933), 6:84.

Personal Learning Activities

1. Although Peter was the author of 1 Peter, _____ served as his secretary. (Choose the correct answer from the list.)
   (1) Mark   (3) John
   (2) Silvanus   (4) James
2. The people to whom Peter wrote lived in an area of the world called Europe. True_____ False_____
3. Probably, the churches that received Peter's letter were composed of _____. (Select the proper response from the list.)
   (1) Jews   (3) Jews and Gentiles
   (2) Romans   (4) Gentiles
4. First Peter is a distinctive kind of writing. From the list, select the appropriate description of the letter.
   ____(1) A persecution document ____(3) A theological work
   ____(2) A friendly letter   ____(4) A gospel
5. In his salutation, Peter prayed that his readers might experience _____ and _____. (Choose the correct answers from the list.)
   (1) Love   (3) Peace
   (2) Grace   (4) Mercy
6. According to Peter, Christians' living hope begins with their determination to reform their lives. True_____ False _____

Answers:
1. (2); 2. False; 3. (3); 4. (1); 5. (2), (3); 6. False.

"Buckle Up," the Best Is Yet to Be

1 Peter 1:13-25

> For without belittling the courage with which men
> have died, we should not forget those acts of courage
> with which men . . . have lived. The courage of life is
> often a less dramatic spectacle than the courage of a
> final moment; but it is not less a magnificent mixture of
> triumph and tragedy. A man does what he must—in
> spite of personal consequences, in spite of obstacles
> and dangers and pressures—and that is the basis of all
> human morality.[1]

Almost four miles above the Atlantic Ocean, my wife Rosalind and I were flying home with a tour group from a visit to the Bible lands. The itinerary had been quite a pilgrimage for us. We had walked for the first time where Jesus had walked—and we felt his presence near! For Rosalind, the trip had been a return to the land of her birth and early childhood. Her parents had been Southern Baptist missionaries in Palestine, but they were called home in 1941 as the World War II conflict moved into the Middle East.

But Bethlehem, Nazareth, Jerusalem, and Galilee now were far behind us. We were glad to be going home. After three weeks of travel, we were looking forward to seeing our children.

Our relaxed in-flight luncheon suddenly was interrupted by the pilot's voice on the intercom. He was saying that we were approaching some turbulence. He suggested that everyone be seated and that all seat belts be fastened. We buckled up immediately.

The next few minutes were the worst air flight experience I have known. The turbulence was severe. The entire plane seemed to start vibrating. Glancing out a side window, I remember thinking that the big plane's wings looked like they were flapping. The dishes on the luncheon trays began to fall into our laps and onto the floor. I tried not to think of our altitude. Any moment, I expected a part of our plane to rip off or to rip open. We could not survive such an accident. What would happen to our children? A real, gut-level panic began to rise in me.

In three or four minutes—which seemed much, much longer—our plane suddenly became steadier. The frightening vibrations stopped, and the wings were not flapping any more. The luncheon dishes on our serving trays rested again. Rosalind and I breathed a deep sigh of relief.

Later, we learned that we had crossed a high altitude jet stream of air moving north to south. Since we were flying east to west, our plane cut directly across the grain or current of this jet stream. In such instances, turbulence always is severe, but seldom disastrous. Needless to say, we were grateful that we had "buckled up" and ridden the turbulence through safely.

My recounting this personal incident gives us a valid, miniature analogy for considering 1 Peter 1:13-25. The author had warned his readers that they were facing some turbulent times. Now, he would counsel them further regarding what he believed would help them to go safely through their time of trial. In essence, in the next paragraphs Peter seemed to indicate something like this: Buckle up! You have some rough times in front of you. You need to be ready to cope with them and to endure them. However, this stress will pass, and you will discover that the best of the Christian life is yet to be!

Strengthen Your Mind-set (1:13)

A hinge word, "therefore," opens 1:13-25 of Peter's letter. This "therefore" refers to everything that Peter had written up to verse 13. In effect, he meant: Because of or in light of all this, . . . we now must do these things.

Peter's first counsel concerned mental attitude. He wrote: "Therefore gird up your minds" (v. 13). The imagery behind this statement was graphic; it referred to the men's style of dress at this

26

time. Rather than wearing today's western-world-style business suits with coat and trousers, the men wore long robes. When they were engaged in strenuous work, they tied their robes up around their waists or "loins" (KJV). This freed their bodies for movement.

The author took a physical-world metaphor and applied it to the mind and the spirit. He encouraged his readers to improve their mental attitudes. Peter did not endorse mental flabbiness among the believers. He did not want them to allow their non-Christian neighbors to be able to think circles around them. With the same thrust of the phrase "gird up your minds," Peter later wrote: "Always be prepared to make a defense to any one who calls you to account for the hope that is in you" (3:15).

Translating the metaphor into today's language, we might say: Roll up your sleeves and get with it! This call obviously was for Christians to be ready to do some hard thinking about their faith. Peter was not for naivete in one's Christian belief. He wanted Christians to know whom, what, and why they had believed.

To think through our faith seriously is still a major Christian task in the church. This means that, at times, we must be unashamedly "theological." In each successive generation, Christians must wrestle with the issues of their day and seek to interpret and apply the gospel to the areas of critical need. "The church is the community in which Christ's mind is being formed and his truth is taken seriously; the church is a high community of rigorous thinking on the part of those who have girded up the loins of their minds."[2] Such life in the church calls more for a courage to live out the faith than to die for the faith.

As a further part of this strengthened mind-set for Christians, Peter urged his readers to "be sober" (v. 13). This counsel did not refer to drinking habits. Rather, it referred to mental attitudes. The admonition meant: Keep calm. The word translated "be sober" (the Greek has only one word) in this context meant to be sensible or to think clearly. We might translate it into modern-day speech like this: Don't lose your cool. Such advice always is sound counsel during a crisis.

A third dimension of the new Christian mind-set looks to the future. Peter wrote: "Set up your hope fully upon the grace that is coming to you at the revelation of Jesus Christ" (v. 13). He firmly believed that Christians should face the future with courageous hope. Therefore, the Christian's hallmark should not be one of despair, but one of hope. This hope should focus on the confident assurance that God will complete the work that he started in Christ. This will take place at the end of time with the "revelation of Jesus Christ"—not as the carpenter from Galilee, but as the risen, reigning Lord.

Straighten Out Your Life-style (1:14-17)

Be Obedient Children (1:14)
We should note that Peter quickly added that the matter of "buckling up" to endure a time of stress involved more than just an improved mental attitude. Our Christian faith demands that we do more than just think about it. Faith in Christ calls for a radical change in life-style. Valid faith in Christ must be acted out on the plane of day-to-day living. We need to think through our faith, but we also need to live it out in daily practice.

Consequently, Peter admonished his readers to be "obedient" (v. 14a). The call to Christian discipleship summons each believer to a new burst of freedom. But Christian freedom never is interpreted as being a state of unrestricted license in which anything goes. Discipleship demands that one submit to the lordship of Christ.

Even in verse 14, Christian obedience was not set in the context of cold, legal codes but in the atmosphere of warm, loving relationships. Peter put Christian obedience in the context of good parent-child relationships within the family—"as obedient *children*" (v. 14), he wrote. His phrase is complimentary, not condescending. Christians "live by no human ideal, nor do they strain to obey cold commandments. Obedience is to a gracious Person, and in doing his good pleasure men will find their highest joy and peace."[3]

Peter defined believers' filial obedience in terms of positive and negative aspects of a Christian life-style. He first stated what Christians were not to do: "Do not be conformed to the passions of your former ignorance" (v. 14b). J. B. Phillips translates this verse: "Don't let your character be molded by the desires of your ignorant days."[4] This meant that they were not to relapse into the bad habits they had possessed when they were pagans.

Peter's admonition in verse 14b is one of several points of internal evidence which seems to indicate that 1 Peter was addressed primarily to a Gentile audience. In light of the revelation that God had given through Moses and the Torah, that a Jewish audience could plead "ignorance" of the kind of behavior which God expected from his people is not likely. The verse seems much more suited to people who came from a predominantly Gentile background. Peter's statement is similar to lines from some of Paul's letters in which he referred to widespread immoral indulgence in physical appetites which characterized much of the Gentile world at that time (Eph. 4:17-20; Phil. 3:17-19; Col. 3:5-6). Obedient Christians were not to live in this way.

Be Holy (1:15-16)

Having stated the matter in terms of what Christians should stop doing, Peter affirmed what should be involved in living a Christian life-style: "But as he who called you is holy, be holy yourselves in all your conduct" (v. 15). The call to Christian discipleship is a call to live a distinctive kind of life—to live a "holy" life.

Sometime ago, I was talking with a group of younger children about the meaning of the word *holy*. I thought that I would compare two words from our church talk which have identical sounds but different meanings. The words were *wholly* and *holy*. When I asked the children if they had any idea about the meaning of these words, one little boy answered. "My brother's socks," he said, "are holely."

Most of us readily would know that **wholly** means *entirely or fully—with nothing held in reserve*. But what is the meaning of the word *holy*?

The term *holy* is one of the basic words in the Bible—both in the Old Testament and in the New Testament. In fact, it is the word which most often is used as a descriptive adjective in referring to the Bible's entire message. Examine the title page of the Bible you are using now and see if you do not find these words: The Holy Bible.

Holiness is a primary attribute of God. The great statesman-prophet Isaiah used this term as a vital part of God's distinctive name: "Thus said the Lord God, the Holy One of Israel" (Isa. 30:15). The basic meaning of the word **holy** is *to be set apart*. We refer to the spirit of this word when we speak of someone or something as being dedicated or consecrated to God's service.

God is holy, and he demands that his people be like him. The goal of being like God never is realized in this life, but the effort to reach it always must be made.

In verse 16, Peter strengthened his appeal for holiness with a quotation from the Old Testament: "You shall therefore be holy, for I am holy" (Lev. 11:45). This statement is in the larger context of a priestly discussion of clean and unclean animals (Lev. 11:1-47). In that setting, the statement seems to deal primarily with dietary regulations, which would imply a concern for ceremonial cleanness or holiness. Later Jewish prophets were to emphasize a holy life-style primarily in terms of moral and ethical standards rather than ritualistic or ceremonial standards.

Thus, we may say that Peter's counsel was more prophetic than it was priestly. His call for a holy life-style did not relate primarily to matters of food and diet. Peter was concerned more with holiness in all his readers' conduct (v. 15b). The Greek word in verse 15b means *turning about—up and down, back and forth.* Thus, Peter was calling Christians to be holy in their total manner of life.

Live in Awe (1:17)

Peter's all-inclusive call is echoed again in his next statement: "And if you invoke as Father him who judges each one impartially according to his deeds, conduct yourselves with fear throughout the time of your exile" (v. 17). Several interesting observations can be made about this exhortation. For example, this may be an early reference to the use of the Lord's Prayer in Christian worship and devotion—"if you invoke as Father." In Luke's Gospel, the model prayer begins simply, "Father, . . ." (11:2). First Peter 1:17 describes God as one "who judges each one impartially." This sounds much like Peter's comment to the Roman centurion, Cornelius (Acts 10:34), when Peter had gone to share with Cornelius and his household the good news of Christ.

But the main thrust of the statement in verse 17 calls further for ethical conduct. Because God will hold Christians accountable for their deeds, they should live holy lives. Peter used an imperative verb tense when he wrote: "Conduct yourselves with fear throughout the time of your exile." In verse 17, **fear** means *with a sense of awe* or *in an attitude of reverence.* In this context, **exile** means *an entire lifetime* or *the total pilgrimage of life.* In a sense, Christians are exiles who live in this world temporarily. As long as a person lives, that individual is to live with a sense of awe concerning the gift of life.

Remember Who Redeemed You (1:18-21)

You Were Ransomed by Christ (1:18-19)

Continuing his appeal for courage in the face of increasingly difficult times, Peter urged his friends to remember how they had gotten to where they were in their Christian faith. "You know," he wrote, "that you were ransomed from the futile ways inherited from your fathers" (v. 18a).

The word *ransom* came from the slave markets of Peter's day. The term referred to the price which was paid to redeem a person; that is, to change one's status from slavery to freedom. In the pagan world, this act of emancipation was a rite that sometimes was accompanied by a sacrifice.

The bondage from which the early Christians had been freed was a servitude to "the futile ways inherited from . . . [their] fathers." The Greek word translated "futile" is quite graphic. It pictures "a fumbling, groping life which makes no effective contact with reality and whose mournful verdict at the end must ever be . . . all is vanity."[5] This language points to the probability of a predominantly Gentile audience as the recipients of 1 Peter.

Peter further reminded his friends that the price of their redemption had been paid by something far more valuable than "silver or gold" (v. 18b). Buying and selling human life for coins always was crass and degrading. Peter's readers, however, had been ransomed or redeemed "with the precious blood of Christ" (v. 19a).

The sacrificial figure is more Jewish in background—a probable reference to the Old Testament sacrificial system. The paschal lamb had to be without blemish or flaw. John the Baptist spoke of Jesus as " 'the Lamb of God, who takes away the sin of the world' " (John 1:29). Peter echoed this same sentiment about Jesus' sacrificial death on the cross. The word "blood" (1 Pet. 1:19) refers to Jesus' life given, poured out voluntarily.

God's Purpose Is Eternal (1:20)

Like the author of the Fourth Gospel (John 1:1-3; 17:24), Peter believed that Jesus was destined to fill the role of Redeemer "from the foundation of the world" (v. 20a), that is, from the beginning of time. Christ as Redeemer had been "made manifest," however, "at the end of the times" (v. 20b), that is, "in the days of Herod, king of Judea" (Luke 1:5). Jesus' coming marked the close of one age and the beginning of a new one. Thus, Peter considered the first generation Christians to be recipients of the best good news that people ever had received.

Your Faith and Hope Are in God (1:21)
The price of our ransom, Jesus' death on the cross, was validated by his mighty resurrection. Through the risen Lord, Christians have "confidence in God" (v. 21a). Our "faith and hope" are assured because both are anchored firmly in God (v. 21b). Generally speaking, in the New Testament the term "faith" refers to what God has done in the past. "Hope" is a New Testament word which faces the future, assured that the same God graciously will be active. Thus, Peter was indicating to his Christian friends that they could "buckle up" in order to endure the persecution which they were to encounter, confident indeed that the best was yet to be.

Affirm Your Permanent Identity (1:22-25)

In the last paragraph of 1 Peter 1, the author pointed toward a higher pinnacle of hope and assurance for his Christian friends in Asia Minor. They were experiencing difficult times. Again, note the subheads whereby we have explored the biblical text for this chapter: "Strengthen Your Mind-Set"; "Straighten Out Your Life-Style"; "Remember Who Redeemed You."

In 1:22-25, Peter urged the early Christians to affirm their permanent identity as God's children. J. B. Phillips translated one of the verses in this passage with this strong meaning: "For you are sons of God now; the live, permanent word of the living God has given you his own indestructible heredity" (v. 23).

Love One Another (1:22)
Peter encouraged his readers to affirm their Christian selfhood in at least three ways. First, they were to declare who they were by their obedience to the truth. Peter wrote: "having purified your souls by your obedience to the truth . . ." (v. 22a). The verb **purify** *(hagnizō)* means *to make clean*. To purify one's soul points toward achieving a clean way of life or a holy life-style. The perfect tense of the Greek verb in verse 22 implies that this is something which already had been achieved in the lives of the early Chris-

tians, and its effect still was being felt.

The readers of 1 Peter had cleaned up their lives by obedience to "the truth" (v. 22). The definite article "the" makes this emphatic. "The truth" is the good news of Christ. Coming out of their predominantly pagan backgrounds, the early Christians in Asia Minor had received the truth of the real God made known through his Son, Jesus Christ.

This brings us to a second way in which Peter's friends could affirm their Christian selfhood. In this new "purified" way of life, the believers had been set free from self-centeredness so that they could love one another with a deeper love than would have been possible previously. Peter wrote: "Having purified your souls . . . for a sincere love of the brethren, love one another earnestly from the heart" (v. 22).

Again, note that Peter's understanding of holiness or being pure was more prophetic than priestly. His emphasis was not on proper rite or ritual. His concern focused on right behavior. Christians demonstrate their "holiness" by loving one another.

Peter would have liked the folk song of our day which declares that people will know Christians by the Christians' love. In the brief verse (22), he used two different Greek verbs for love. "Love of the brethren" is just one word in the original—the same word which gives us the name *Philadelphia*, City of "Brotherly Love." The verb *phileō*, from which the noun *philos* comes, is the key word here. It refers to the strong bond of love between friends.

When Peter wrote, "Love one another earnestly from the heart" (v. 22), however, he used another Greek word, *agapēsate*, from agapaō. This word refers to the kind of love which God has for us—unmerited, spontaneous, and undying. Paul described this love as the highest Christian virtue (1 Cor. 13). He wrote: "So faith, hope, love abide, these three: but the greatest of these is love" (1 Cor. 13:13). Note that Peter had this same trilogy—faith, hope, and love—in close proximity (vv. 21-22).

You Have Been Born Anew (1:23*a*)
Peter suggested a third way whereby the early Christians could affirm their permanent identity. Of the three ways he mentioned, the most important clearly referred to what God had done for the believers and not to what they were called to do themselves.

Note carefully Peter's line of thought at this point. He declared again his belief in the initial, new-birth experience of redemption:

33

"You have been born anew" (v. 23a). You will recall that Peter already had used this metaphor in the opening lines of his letter (v. 3). However, in verse 23 he used a different verb tense—the perfect tense. This referred to something which had happened in the past, and the effects of this occurrence continued to be known. For Peter, the new birth in Christian conversion was far more than just a temporary, emotional high. It was a life-changing experience which continued to affect the believer's whole life as the years unfolded.

You Have Heard the Good News (1:23b-25)

Equally true for Peter was the fact that the new birth was a spiritual experience in which something indelible and indestructible took place in the believer's life. Reminiscent of Jesus' parable of the sower (Matt. 13:3-9,18-23), Peter described the new birth in terms of seed being planted in the believer's heart. However, rather than being perishable or mortal like most seed, this seed continued to be imperishable or immortal (v. 23b).

Then Peter identified the indestructible seed as "the living and abiding word of God" (v. 23c). Peter quoted a statement from the Old Testament prophet Isaiah which contrasted the transiency of human life and of most plant life with the enduring nature of God's Word: " 'All flesh is like grass and all its glory like the flower of grass. The grass withers and the flower falls, but the word of the Lord abides for ever" (vv. 24-25a; also see Isa. 40:6-9).

On the basis of such reasoning, Peter drew his clinching conclusion: "That word is the good news which was preached to you" (v. 25). In other words, God's eternal Word which Isaiah wrote about is the same good news of Christ. This "truth" (v. 22) purifies the souls of believers and sets them free from sin and selfishness so that they truly may love one another.

In various ways, we have seen how Peter encouraged his readers to remain loyal to their Christian faith even in times of great stress and difficulty. He was convinced that the troubled times would pass and that those who weathered the storm would emerge to receive an indestructible inheritance from God through Jesus Christ.

Martin Luther knew times of great stress as a Christian. He echoed the same confident faith in these lines from his great Reformation hymn, "A Mighty Fortress Is Our God":

Let goods and kindred go, This mortal life also;

The body they may kill: God's truth abideth
  still,
  His kingdom is forever.

So Peter, Martin Luther, and countless multitudes of other faithful Christians who have endured hard times would say to our generation: "Buckle up! The best is yet to be."

Lessons for Life from 1 Peter 1:13-25

In order to survive and carry on a redemptive ministry, Christians still need a firm mind-set.—Like the ballast in a ship, a steady mind-set keeps Christians from keeling over in a storm. Like the rudder of a ship, a strong mind-set keeps Christians headed in the right direction. Like a spiritual gyroscope, a healthy mind-set helps Christians maintain a proper balance and priority in a topsy-turvy world. Such a firm mind-set is not inflexible dogmatism. Instead, it includes the ability to think clearly in the face of difficult problems and to maintain real poise and calm even under pressure. It allows one to keep a sense of vision which looks to the future knowing that the difficult problems also will pass—as God leads his dear children along.

As in the first century, our time calls for deep thought and direct action in demonstrating a genuine Christian life-style.—Our Christian faith is more than something that we think about; it is something which we do. Abstract thought must become concrete actions in specific situations. The action merely may be our giving a cup of cold water in Jesus' name, but the deed must accompany the dogma.

Christian faith should help us to work through what is sometimes called identity crises which many contemporary people experience.—When they are asked: Will the real you please stand up? many people do not know which side of their personalities to present. Peter believed that through Christ, the living God gave all believers a part of "His own indestructible heredity" (1:23, Phillips). Christians are God's sons and daughters. As a mark of this identity, believers should be obedient children. They should love one another. They should rejoice in the new birth which has made them an undeniable part of God's family. Knowing who we are as Christians always should be a source of strength and courage. We are God's children for whom he cares.

1. John F. Kennedy, *Profiles in Courage* (New York: Harper & Bros.: Pub., 1955), p. 246.
2. Elmer G. Homrighausen, *The Interpreter's Bible* (Nashville: Abingdon Press, 1957), 12:100*b*.
3. Homrighausen, p. 101*b*.
4. Reprinted with permission of Macmillan Publishing Co., Inc. from J. B. Phillips: The New Testament in Modern English, Revised Edition. © J. B. Phillips 1958, 1960, 1972. Subsequent quotations are marked Phillips.
5. Archibald M. Hunter, *The Interpreter's Bible*, 12:102.

Personal Learning Activities

1. Peter admonished his readers to conduct themselves as _____ _____. (Select the correct answer from the list.)
   (1) Faithful servants   (3) Obedient children
   (2) Honest employees   (4) Courageous soldiers
2. Evidence exists in 1 Peter that the letter was addressed primarily to a _____ audience in the churches. (Choose the proper answer from the list.)
   (1) Jewish   (3) Samaritan
   (2) Roman   (4) Gentile
3. Peter used a word from the slave market of his day to write of what Christ had done for believers. From the list, choose the proper answer.
   ____(1) Purchased   (3) Bargained
   ____(2) Ransomed   (4) Bartered
4. Match the lists by pairing the terms with their correct definitions.
   ____(1) Faith   (a) Converted
   ____(2) Hope   (b) To love like God
   ____(3) Truth   (c) Bond between friends
   ____(4) Love of the   (d) The good news
            brethren   (e) Assurance of the future
   ____(5) *Agapaō*   (f) Trust based on the past
   ____(6) Born anew

Answers:
1. (3); 2. (4); 3. (2); 4. (1)f, (2)e, (3)d, (4)c, (5)b, (6)a.

36

3

Our Firm Foundation
Is in Jesus Christ

1 Peter 2:1-10

My hope is built on nothing less
Than Jesus' blood and righteousness;
I dare not trust the sweetest frame,
But wholly lean on Jesus' name.

On Christ, the solid Rock, I stand;
All other ground is sinking sand.

—Edward Mote
"The Solid Rock"

Following graduation from the seminary, I was happy to become pastor of the First Baptist Church, Hope, Arkansas. Located in the southwest corner of my home state, this county seat has achieved some fame as the watermelon capital of the world. The world's largest watermelons on record have been grown in this area, with the prize-winning melons usually weighing over two hundred pounds.

When my family and I arrived in Hope, we found the congregation enjoying the use of a new sanctuary. The red-brick, Georgian Colonial structure was a beautiful, spacious building. Of particular interest to me was the towering church spire, which rose from the front of the building above the four massive white columns. This spire could be seen from some distance away as a person drove into this small town.

In talking with some of the church members, I learned that

37

when construction plans for a new sanctuary initially began, quite a discussion had taken place about the possibility of having a spire. Many people wanted a colonial building with a towering spire, but some authorities said that it was not architecturally feasible at that specific site. Longtime residents of Hope knew that the immediate area of the church's location once had been an old "pin oak flat." The texture of the soil in such terrain would not support a tall church spire, so some thought.

A determined group of people, however, made plans for a thorough foundation for the new building. As preparation was made for erecting the spire, heavy-duty pile-driving equipment was brought to the site. Piling was driven through the layers of gray clay in the pin oak flat to reach a firm footing far beneath the surface of the earth. The Georgian Colonial building was crowned with a beautiful spire. Local people who were aware of the soil condition were delighted that at the time no cracks had appeared in the building. The carefully engineered foundation was holding secure.

Not long after the church was completed, a public utility company made plans to construct a new building just across the street. This building was designed to be both office space and heavy equipment storage space for the utility company. Out-of-town engineers and construction people were engaged to do this project. Some local citizens tried to counsel these builders about the soil condition and the old pin oak flat. For some reason, however, their counsel was not heeded. The foundation for this building had no deep-level piling base.

During the years that my family and I lived in Hope, the church building with the towering spire remained fully intact. The utility building across the street, however, literally began to fall apart. Gaping cracks appeared in the walls and the floors of this building. At great additional expense, company officials had to come in with a plan to try to keep this building from collapsing.

Anyone who saw these two structures just across the street from each other became aware of the vital importance of an adequate foundation. For years, construction people have said that the most important part of any building is that which goes beneath the ground. Here in reality, a person could see the difference that a strong foundation makes in keeping a building intact and erect.

As we come to 1 Peter 2:1-10, we will learn that the apostle wrote about the importance of an adequate foundation for life.

Peter declared that a solid rock exists on which we may stand—the chief cornerstone, Jesus Christ.

First Peter's overall theme will become more apparent as we move into 1 Peter 2. You will recall that we have described the letter as a message of encouragement which emphasized the Christian life-style. In 1 Peter 2, Peter declared that a Christian life-style involves three important concerns: (1) growing up to salvation, (2) building on the cornerstone, and (3) becoming God's people.

Growing Up to Salvation (2:1-3)

In the first chapter of this textbook, we noted that the word "salvation" was used in the New Testament in at least three different ways. It may refer to the initial experience of receiving Christ as Savior and Lord. Or, it may refer to the ultimate consummation of salvation, when God receives a person into his heavenly home. We noted that this was the use of the word in 1 Peter 1:9.

A third use of the word salvation referred to the process of growing in Christian maturity. In this latter sense, Peter used the term in 2:2. He did not question whether the believers were born-again Christians. Twice he had referred to them as having been "born anew" (1:3,23). He was convinced that they had known the initial salvation experience. Evidently, they had not had sufficient time and opportunity to grow in the salvation experience. Peter's next appeal focused at this point.

Discarding Negatives (2:1)

Peter began by asking the Christians to "put away" (2:1) some specific patterns of attitude and behavior. Again, similar exhortations may be found in Paul's letters (Eph. 4:22-25; Col. 3:8). The metaphor of this verb refers to changing one's clothing. An old set of garments is put off or put away in order that a new set of garments may be put on.

Peter was indicating that Christian conversion involved a change. More than just a change in wardrobe, however, this was a basic change in life-style. Also, the time-frame in Christian conversion is extended more. Whereas we put away clothes for a season, Peter wanted his new Christian friends to put away some old behavior patterns for a lifetime. He mentioned five specific traits which the believers were to put away: "all malice and guile and insincerity and envy and all slander" (v. 1).

The word "malice" was a general, all-inclusive term for wickedness of all kinds. In a sense, this umbrella word includes the other four traits which Peter listed. Malice may be expressed both in word and in deed. James used the same word in his statement, "Therefore put away all filthiness and rank growth of wickedness" (1:21).

"Guile" is a word which points to the role of deceit in human relationships. The noun came from a verb stem which meant to catch or hook with a bait. Such deceit or guile allows an individual to manipulate other people for selfish gain in whatever manner he or she wishes.

The word translated in verse 1 as **insincerity** is a form of the Greek word which also means *hypocrite*. Initially such a person was one who answered. In time, the word came to be associated primarily with the stage, so that a hypocrite was one who answered from behind a mask as he or she played a role in a drama. Still later, the word became identified with playacting off the stage. A **hypocrite** was *one who spoke from behind a mask,* never honestly revealing his or her true motives. The hypocrite is a fake, an imposter, a phony.

Envy *is the sinister attitude of resentment toward another person who has excelled or been particularly blessed.* It follows in the wake of a passionate egotism which cannot allow other people to succeed without incurring red coals of smoldering hostility.

The word translated **slander** literally means *evil speakings.* Our everyday language would say backbiting or gossip. Such language often is the verbal eruption of what envy has done in the heart.

Peter declared that none of the traits was included in the dress code for Christians. Persons who brought such attitudes or patterns of behavior from their pagan backgrounds were to put away this kind of life-style. The verb **put away** also can mean *strip off.* Peter wrote that these negative traits were to be "peeled off" and thrown away, never to be picked up again, as when one is eating a banana and strips off the peel.

Desiring the Best (2:2-3)
Having indicated some things which the Christians should discard, Peter mentioned something for which they should yearn:

"Like newborn babes, long for the pure spiritual milk, that by it you may grow up to salvation" (v. 2).

Peter again used the figure of birth to describe the Christians' new state. His specific word was the Greek term which referred to the youngest type of infant—a babe in arms.

Peter's emphasis was not on the newness of birth. Instead, he pointed to a nursing baby's hunger drive. Hunger can be a strong force in any person's life, in people's quest for survival. The hunger drive is an almost all-consuming force in an infant's life. In this sense, hunger is one of the most basic of all human drives.

Peter took the figure of the newborn baby from the physical world and applied it to Christian living. As newborn babies hunger for their mother's milk, so Peter urged the new Christian converts to "long for the pure spiritual milk" (v. 2). His words remind us of one of Jesus' Beatitudes: " 'Blessed are those who hunger and thirst for righteousness, for they shall be satisfied' " (Matt. 5:6).

The word **pure** in verse 2 means undiluted or unadulterated. This Greek adjective was formed from the noun meaning deceit with the addition of an alpha privative. The literal meaning was without deceit, or with no deceit.

The word translated "spiritual" is the same Greek word which gives us our word "logical." Paul used this word in his Letter to the Romans (12:1) to describe the kind of service or worship which Christians are to give to God. Paul also used the word "milk" to refer to instruction in the most elementary things of the Christian faith (1 Cor. 3:2).

For the Christians, the milk or source of nourishment to which Peter referred was God's Word. Newborn babies have a strong drive to eat in order that they may grow. In like manner, Peter urged the new converts to nourish their fledgling Christian lives on God's Word so that they might grow.

Peter also made specific the direction of the believer's growth. The new Christians were to "grow up to salvation" (v. 2); they were to move from being babes in the faith to become more mature adult persons in the Christian faith. Thus, Peter saw salvation as being an initial act of responsive faith and a process of growth toward God's intended goal.

Peter's concluding phrase in the paragraph 2:1-3 of his letter gave a reason why the new Christians should know a strong hunger for God's word: "for you have tasted the kindness of the

41

Lord" (v. 3). This is not the first biblical exhortation using the sense of taste in reference to God. For example, the psalmist had written: "O taste and see that the Lord is good" (34:8)!

In the Scriptures, the word **taste** meant more than just to take a sip. For instance, Jesus used the word in referring to certain persons' experiencing death (Mark 9:1). Today, we may speak of someone having a close brush with death. The New Testament use of "taste," however, did not refer to such a close encounter. **To taste** of death actually meant *to die.*

Thus, when Peter wrote of Christians as having "tasted" of the Lord, he meant that they had known fully an experience of God through Jesus Christ. They had found that taste to be most pleasant. God was, and still is, kind and good.

Today, we often speak of acquiring a taste for some new food so that we develop a hunger or craving for that particular dish. About such a food we may say: I just can't seem to get enough of that! Peter did not hesitate to use this graphic metaphor to describe how the new Christians should desire to know more and more of God in Jesus Christ.

Building on the Cornerstone (2:4-8)

As Peter continued to exhort his friends to live the committed Christian life-style, he moved his metaphor from the feeding habits of children to the building of a house of worship. In making this change, he picked up imagery from one of Jesus' parables (Matt. 21:42). In the parable of the vineyard and the tenants, Jesus identified himself as the chief cornerstone. He used Psalm 118:22, which Peter also used in his letter. The verses in 1 Peter (2:4-8) pictured what God intended for life together in the church to be.

Come to the Living Stone (2:4,6-7)
You will note that verse 4 begins a new paragraph in the Revised Standard Version. Peter had mentioned that the new Christians had tasted the Lord's kindness. Now he wrote, "Come to him" (v. 4). The verb form is a present tense participle which denotes durative action. In context, this transition might read like this: "Since you have tasted the kindness of the Lord, keep on coming to him."

The Revised Standard Version also translates the participle as

an imperative, in parallel mood with another verb form in the passage. We usually punctuate imperative statements with an exclamation mark. All of this means that Peter's language reflects a genuine sense of excitement about coming to Jesus. He obviously thought that repeated behavior of this kind was important. He immediately proceeded to indicate why he believed this.

As we have indicated, Peter borrowed a metaphor which Jesus had used of himself. Peter identified Jesus as "that living stone, rejected by men but in God's sight chosen and precious" (v. 4). At this point, to read Jesus' parable of the vineyard owner and the tenants will be helpful (Matt. 21:33-43).

Likely, Jesus and Peter were referring to a traditional story which was told about building the Temple in Jerusalem. During the early construction, the builders had rejected a certain unusually shaped stone. Later, however, they discovered that they needed a stone of that specific size and shape. The rejected stone then became the most needed and essential stone for the erection of the Temple.

In addition to Psalm 118:22 (v. 7), Peter also quoted from Isaiah 28:16 in making his point. The great statesman-prophet of Jerusalem had written words which Peter described as "scripture" (v. 6):

"Behold, I am laying in Zion a
stone, a cornerstone chosen and precious,
and he who believes in him will
not be put to shame.' "

In current building practices, laying a cornerstone for a building usually is one of the last items of brick-and-mortar work to be done. Placing the cornerstone often is associated with the inauguration of a building for public use. Today, laying a cornerstone is primarily a formality.

In Bible times, however, a cornerstone played a much more essential role in construction. Like the keystone in a natural stone archway, the cornerstone filled a basic place in holding up the connecting walls of a building. Buildings of that era had no internal steel or concrete supports. External walls were not veneer; they were load-bearing. Without an adequate cornerstone, such walls would not stand. As loose stones in walls shifted, a building collapsed.

In using the cornerstone metaphor, Peter was affirming that Christ is the essential foundation for life. The Jewish religious leaders of Jesus' day rejected him. But in God's sight, he was not repudiated. Instead, he remained "chosen and precious" (v. 4). Although many of Jesus' peers counted him worthless, God regarded him as supremely honorable and worthy.

We also should note that Peter called Jesus a "living stone" (v. 4). Earlier, he had affirmed the "living hope" (1:3) which Christians have through Jesus' resurrection from the dead. He had written of the "living . . . word" of God (1:23) as the source or seed of Christians' indestructible inheritance. Now, in contrast to the cold, dead building stones, Peter described Jesus as a cornerstone who was alive. Peter saw Jesus as the living One who had conquered death and as the life-giving One who will sustain all who lean on him.

Become Living Stones (2:5,8)

The idea of Jesus as the living cornerstone formed the basis for Peter's next appeal: "Come to him, to that living stone, . . . and like living stones be yourselves built into a spiritual house" (vv. 4-5). Not only did Peter see Jesus as a living stone, the chief cornerstone; he also saw the Christians in Asia Minor as being living stones which were to be built into a spiritual house. The key word in verse 5 is that same verb which Jesus used when he told Peter: "On this rock I will build my church" (Matt. 16:18).

By referring to the believers as living stones, Peter obviously did not think of the church primarily in terms of brick and mortar. For Peter and for Jesus, the church first of all was people. Neither of them had an edifice complex (a compulsion to erect buildings) in describing the church.

Lawrence T. Lowrey, longtime president of Blue Mountain College in Mississippi, had an interesting reply which he gave to visitors who came to his campus during the summer months. Blue Mountain did not have a summer session at that time. Off-campus visitors often would greet Dr. Lowrey like this: "We've driven by to see the college."

This was the president's standard reply: "We are happy to have you at Blue Mountain, but I regret that the college is not here. I can show you some buildings and the larger campus; but the college has gone home for the summer!"

Dr. Lowrey knew that first of all, a college is students. In like fashion, Jesus and Peter indicated that the church is people.

Peter defined two tasks which God's people were to accomplish. First, they were to be "a holy priesthood" (v. 5). Obviously, Peter did not view the priesthood as being a special status for only a select few. All believers were regarded as priests. This is one of the Scriptures which helps to form the biblical foundation for our Baptist doctrine of the priesthood of all Christians.

The word *priest*, of course, has been used by many different religions and cultures. It generally refers to a person who is considered to have open access to God and who seeks to represent both himself and other people before God. The Latin word for priest, **pontifex,** is especially graphic. The word means *bridge-builder*. This concept seems to fit Peter's idea expressed in verse 5. All Christians were to have ready access to God, and they were to be ministers of reconciliation—bridge builders—between other people and God.

Both in Judaism and in the Gentile religions, in their approach to God priests primarily had made animal sacrifices. Peter declared that Christians no longer were to make such sacrifices. He believed that Christians had been "ransomed . . . with the precious blood of Christ" (1:18-19). He thus reflected the same belief which we find in the Letter to the Hebrews, that Christ has "once for all" paid the price of redemption for those persons who believe in his death on the cross (Heb. 7:27; 9:12; 10:10).

Peter mentioned a second task that God's people were to accomplish. He defined the sacrifices which Christians were to make as "spiritual sacrifices" (v. 5). His thought is similar to Paul's in Romans 12:1. **Spiritual sacrifices** meant that *believers brought themselves to God*. They offered their work and their worship as expressions of love and obedience to God. Such personal, spiritual sacrifices were acceptable to God through Jesus Christ (v. 5).

We should note one other thought which Peter mentioned about Jesus as the chief cornerstone. As we have seen, for those who receive Jesus as Savior and Lord, he becomes a firm foundation and a source of great strength. For those who do not receive him, he becomes a stone of judgment. Peter again quoted from Isaiah:

"A stone that will make men
   stumble,
 a rock that will make them fall." (v. 8; see Isa.
   8:14-15).

Most pupils do not like to take final exams. Neither do people like the idea of being judged, being held accountable. However, Peter had arrived at the idea of redemption and the idea of judgment in his understanding of who Jesus was. He indicated that the reason people stumble on the cornerstone is "because they disobey the word, as they were destined to do" (v. 8). The latter phrase does not mean predestined in the sense that those people had no choice as to what response they would make to God's word. The choice was theirs, and they made it. But to reject and disobey, as some did, brought a destiny of judgment.

Becoming God's Own People (2:9-10)

Now we come to the third major concern which Peter defined as a vital part of the Chrisian life-style. Again, his understanding of the Christian life included specific acts or deeds and a dynamic process.

We have seen that Peter applied the metaphor of birth and the metaphor of growth to the Christian life, as though they were two sides of the same coin. In like manner, he discussed the importance of having a firm foundation as well as the importance of erecting a strong building on the foundation.

In this same line of thought, Peter dealt with the matters of being and becoming. Believers in Jesus Christ already were God's people; yet in maturing discipleship, they should have been becoming more fully God's people. In each of these transitions, Peter's language implied an initial act of faith and a continuing development of that faith.

Chosen for a Purpose (2:9)
Peter first used four well-known Old Testament titles for Israel and applied them to the young churches in Asia Minor. The four titles may have been four points in one of Peter's sermons on the nature of the church. He wrote: "But you are a chosen race, a royal priesthood, a holy nation, God's own people" (v. 9).

God's choice of Israel was a familiar idea expressed by the Old Testament writers. For example, the author of Deuteronomy declared: "Yet the Lord set his heart in love upon your fathers and chose their descendants after them, you above all peoples, as at this day" (10:15, my italics).

Moses had described old Israel as "a kingdom of priests and a holy nation" (Ex. 19:6). His words were echoed in Deuteronomy: "The Lord has declared this day concerning you . . . that you shall be a people holy to the Lord your God" (26:18-19).

The first three Old Testament titles in 1 Peter 2:9 point toward God's electing grace in choosing Israel for a unique role in his salvation plan for mankind. God chose Israel, not because of the people's merit, but out of the spontaniety of his redeeming love. In their service for the one, true, sovereign God, they were like a royal priesthood. They became a holy, separated people, not just by their ceremonial rites and religious observances, but also by their keeping the covenant and by their superior moral and ethical behavior.

Peter used the Old Testament figures to declare that Christians now were fulfilling Israel's role and vocation. The church was to be the New Israel, with the same kind of calling which had been given to Old Israel.

The title "God's own people" (v. 9) also had strong roots in the Old Testament. You should note the footnote for this title in the Revised Standard Version, "a people for his possession." This phrase was a direct reference from God's promise to Israel when the Mosaic covenant was established at Sinai. At that time, God said to Israel: "If you will obey my voice and keep my covenant, you shall be my own possession among all peoples; for all the earth is mine" (Ex. 19:5, my italics).

The original language referred to a special treasure which the owner cherished. In a real sense, a reigning monarch was the owner of everything in his realm. From the personal, human viewpoint, when one owned all, nothing was special. Consequently, kings of that time developed a practice of having some special treasures which were uniquely their own cherished possessions. God, who owned all the earth, held Israel as this kind of prized possession.

The practice of keeping a special treasure became the fourth Old Testament figure which Peter used to describe God's relationship to the church. As Israel once had been God's special treasure, the church now filled this role in his special concern.

Peter declared that the significant titles or roles did not imply the use of God's favor for selfish ends. As old Israel had been called to a witnessing, serving role, so the church also was asked to "declare the wonderful deeds of him who called you out of darkness into his marvelous light" (v. 9).

The four titles with their strong Old Testament background might seem to imply that 1 Peter was sent to a Jewish audience. However, the phrase—called out of darkness into light—seemed to point toward the recipients of this letter as being predominantly Gentile. The Bible consistently regarded the Gentiles as people who dwelt in darkness. Coming to God was like coming to the light. (See Isa. 60:1-2.)

From Nobodies to Somebodies (2:10)

The last verse in the passage 2:1-10 poignantly reminds the reader of the moving story of domestic tragedy in the lives of the Old Testament prophet Hosea and his wife Gomer (Hos. 1:1-11; 3:1-5). Through Gomer's unfaithfulness, Hosea learned the deep truth about God's faithfulness. People who had made themselves *nobodies* could be *somebodies* in God's forgiving grace. Peter borrowed directly from Hosea's writing (Hos. 2:23) as he encouraged the new Christian converts in Asia Minor: "Once you were no people but now you are God's people; once you had not received mercy but now you have received mercy" (v. 10).

Peter declared that God's grace in Christ has transformed all who believe in him into God's persons. So he urged his readers to find a firm foundation for life in Christ. They were to do this by growing up beyond their initial experience of salvation, by building life with Christ as the chief cornerstone, and by being and becoming God's people.

Lessons for Life from 1 Peter 2:1-10

From a Christian viewpoint, salvation is a dynamic, three-dimensional experience.—It originates as the believer initially receives Christ as Savior and Lord. It will be consummated as each believer is received into his or her heavenly home. The salvation experience's major segment, however, takes place between the points of origin and consummation. For most of us, this dimension of salvation encompasses the major part of our lives in terms of longevity. Too many Christians are stillborn at the time of conversion. Although they are genuinely reborn, they never begin the arduous task of growing up and reaching toward maturity in Christ. In both the first and the twentieth centuries, churches need believers as members who were/are growing up to salvation (2:2).

Christ is the one adequate foundation for life.—From the building practices of his day, Peter declared that Christ is the chief cornerstone. Although today's building arts are vastly different from those in Peter's day, Christ is still the only foundation for the good life. Peter would have liked Paul's comment: "For no other foundation can any one lay than that which is laid, which is Jesus Christ" (1 Cor. 3:11).

An authentic Christian life-style embraces the concepts of being and becoming.—In terms of being, as born-again believers we are God's children. In terms of becoming, we always are seeking to move from being newborn babes in Christ to becoming mature men and women in him.

Personal Learning Activities

1. In what three ways is the word *salvation* used in the New Testament?
2. Peter mentioned five traits that his readers were to put away. Name three of the traits.
3. The spiritual milk that Peter exhorted his readers to desire was _____. (Select the proper answer from the list.)
   (1) Fellowship   (3) God's word
   (2) Worship   (4) Friendship
4. In the New Testament, the word **taste** meant *to experience fully.* True_____ False_____
5. For Peter and for Jesus, the church was (choose the correct answer from the list):
   ____(1) A building   (3) People
   ____(2) An organization   (4) A business
6. Peter applied distinctive titles to believers, God's people. From the list, select the proper titles.
   ____(1) A chosen race   (3) A holy nation
   ____(2) A royal priesthood   (4) God's own people

Answers:
1. A past, present, and future experience; 2. Malice, guile, insincerity, envy, and slander; 3. (3); 4. True; 5. (3); 6. All answers.

4

Our Dual Citizenship, Through Jesus Christ

1 Peter 2:11-25

For Christians are not distinguished from the rest of mankind either in locality or in speech or in customs. For they dwell not somewhere in cities of their own, neither do they use some different language. . . . But while they dwell in cities of Greeks and barbarians as the lot of each is cast, and follow the native customs in dress and food and the other arrangements of life, yet the constitution of their own citizenship, which they set forth, is marvellous, and confessedly contradicts expectation. They dwell in their own countries, but only as sojourners; they bear their share in all things as citizens, and they endure all hardships as strangers. Every foreign country is a fatherland to them, and every fatherland is foreign. They marry like all other men and they beget children; but they do not cast away their offspring. They have their meals in common, but not their wives. They find themselves in the flesh, and yet they live not after the flesh. Their existence is on earth, but their citizenship is in heaven.[1]

December 4, 1980 became a red-letter day on our family calendar. On this date, our nine-year-old daughter from Korea became a naturalized citizen of the United States of America. Laura Elizabeth already had been an adopted member of our family for almost five years. She had come directly to our home from Seoul, Korea, as a bright-eyed, dark-haired four year old. My wife and I met Laura Elizabeth in a group of ten other children at O'Hare Field in Chicago on January 14, 1976. That date became "gotcha day" for our family. Now, December 4 is another special occasion: naturalization day.

Naturalization is the legal process by which a person changes his or her citizenship from one country to another. The word **naturalize** literally means *to make natural*. Applied to citizenship, the word refers to the formal act of conferring the rights and privileges of a native-born subject on a person who was born in another country. A person who is being naturalized takes an oath of allegiance pledging loyalty to his or her newly adopted homeland.

A naturalized citizen of the United States has full rights as a citizen, except that he or she cannot be elected President or Vice-President. Naturalized citizens are entitled to full protection by the United States if they travel abroad.

This formal legal process became quite personal for us on the day our adopted daughter became a new American citizen. She was one of over fifty persons who were naturalized on that day. From younger preschool children to older adults, many different ages and natural backgrounds were in the group. Earnest eyes and serious faces seemed to reflect the reverent solemnity of the moment. I found myself thinking of the lines of poetess Emma Lazarus which are inscribed on the pedestal of the Statue of Liberty in New York Harbor:

"Give me your tired, your poor,
Your huddled masses yearning to breathe free,
The wretched refuse of your teeming shore;
Send these, the homeless, tempest-tost to me:
I lift my lamp beside the golden door."

Varying accents were distinct as this international choir recited in unison their pledge of allegiance to the American flag. I winked at our daughter, and suddenly my eyes blurred with tears. I noticed several other people crying unashamedly. It was a soul-stirring time, a day in our family experience which we will remember always.

Peter turned his attention to citizenship concerns in the section 2:11-25 of his letter. After he affirmed their sure inheritance in heaven, he exhorted his Christian friends in the five provinces to live out the demands of their faith on earth. His challenge still speaks to us today.

Maintain a Winsome Life-Style (2:11-12)

First Peter 2:11-12 marks a major shift in Peter's letter. Although this is not the midpoint of the letter contentwise, all that precedes this passage is Part 1, and all that comes afterward is Part 2. The Revised Standard Version acknowledges this basic division in the letter by skipping a line space between verse 10 and verse 11 in chapter 2.

The first part of the letter primarily has been theological in nature. Peter was concerned that his friends should become fully aware of how God had related himself to them in saving grace through Christ. The last part of the letter primarily will be ethical in nature. Peter spelled out what living as a Christian meant in specific areas of daily life with other people.

The transition from theology to ethics is found in other New Testament letters. For example, it may be seen clearly in Paul's Letter to the Romans (12:1) and also in his Letter to the Ephesians (4:1) We should be careful, however, not to make a sharp distinction between theological sections and ethical sections. Probably, neither Peter nor Paul had such categories in mind. "Ethical" guidelines grew naturally out of "theological" or doctrinal matters.

Concern for proper relationships to God and to people is at the heart of the total biblical revelation. The Ten Commandments reflect this approach to religious faith and daily life. The first four Commandments deal with people's relationship to God. The last six Commandments concern people's life in relationship to other persons. When Jesus summarized the Commandments in terms of greatest priority, his answer reflected this twofold distinction: " 'You shall love the Lord your God with all your heart, and with all your soul, and with all your mind. This is the great and first commandment. And a second is like it, You shall love your neighbor as yourself. On these two commandments depend all the law and the prophets' " (Matt. 22:37-40).

So, from Moses to Jesus to Paul, Peter followed the mainstream of the biblical message as he applied the gospel truth to people's total lives. Theology without ethics too easily becomes irrelevant piety. Ethics without theology quickly degenerates into shallow humanism. Theology and ethics together, however, constitute a sound approach. Peter reflected this kind of keen insight as he continued to exhort his friends in Asia Minor.

Abstain from Fleshly Passions (2:11)

Peter began the ethical part of his letter with a warm word of personal endearment. He addressed his readers as "beloved" (v. 11). John often used this tender expression in his correspondence (1 John 3:2,21; 4:1,7). With this affectionate term, Peter seemed to imply that he *and* God loved his readers.

We also should note that in 2:11, Peter used the first person form of address for the first time in his letter. He wrote: "I beseech you" (v. 11). This verb form carried the same mood of personal appeal which was conveyed by the term "beloved." The present tense of this verb implied durative action: Beloved, I keep on beseeching you.

Next, Peter borrowed two words from first-century terminology concerning citizenship and applied them to Christians. The first word, translated "aliens," was used in the Greek to refer to persons living in a foreign country where they had no rights of citizenship. For example, refugees who came to the United States from Vietnam or Cuba would fall into this category. The other word, translated "exiles," emphasized transiency in residence. It referred to a person who was staying temporarily in a country which was not his or her permanent home.

Obviously, Peter believed that Christians never could feel fully at home in this world. Christians live on earth responsibly, but their ultimate home is in heaven. Peter would have agreed with the role of citizenship for Christians expressed in the Epistle to Diognetus: "Every foreign country is a fatherland to them, and every fatherland is foreign."[2]

Peter urged his friends to do some abstaining (v. 11) and some maintaining (v. 12). His word choice pointed to negative and positive dimensions of authentic Christian living. On some occasions, Christians reveal their true nature by what they *choose* to do. At other times, they make themselves known by what they *refuse* to do.

Peter appealed to his readers "to abstain from the passions of the flesh" that waged war against their souls (v. 11). The present tense of both verbs in this verse indicates durative action: Keep on abstaining from the passions of the flesh that keep on waging war against your soul. The idea of Christians being engaged in spiritual warfare was one of Paul's favorite metaphors. One of his best-known passages using this imagery is Ephesians 6:11-17.

Spiritual warfare pits the fleshly or carnal side of persons'

54

nature against the spiritual or soul dimension of their person-hood. To recognize this conflict within people did not commit Peter to a form of psychological dualism. Such a complete dualism is always more Greek than it is Hebrew-Christian. Greek dualism declares that the body is evil and that only the spirit (or soul) is good. In verse 11, Peter simply recognized the dueling nature which exists within each of us.

Maintain Good Conduct (2:12)

Moving to more positive counsel, Peter urged his readers to "maintain good conduct among the Gentiles" (v. 12). The phrase "good conduct" referred to a person's total way of life. Note the King James Version's translation of this phrase: "Having your conversation honest among the Gentiles." In 1611, the words *honest* and *conversation* referred not to the way people talked but to the way they walked. Thus, honest conversation meant upright behavior.

On two earlier occasions in his letter, Peter had used the Greek word which in this verse is translated **conversation** (KJV) or **conduct** (1:15,17). Once, he used a noun form; once, he employed a verb form. The word literally meant *turning about* or *turning upside down*.

The Greek word translated **honest** (KJV) or **good** had a strong ethical connotation. It meant *marked by integrity* or *morally good*. The word also carried the meaning of *being lovely* or *beautiful*. Perhaps *winsome* is the best English word to convey the meaning.

The phrase "among the Gentiles" in verse 12 should not be interpreted to mean that the churches Peter addressed were predominantly Jewish, for **Gentiles** meant the *nations in general*. Such usage was commonplace in the New Testament.

Peter's motive for calling his friends to winsome Christian conduct was to silence their opponents. He specifically wrote: "So that in case they speak against you as wrongdoers, they may see your good deeds and glorify God on the day of visitation" (v. 12).

Strange as the fact may seem to us, first-century Christians often were charged as being wrongdoers. During the Neronian persecution, the Roman author Suetonius used this specific word to refer to Christians. At best, many unbelievers looked on Christians as being pests in the Empire. At worst, Christians were blamed for any unusual, destructive natural event or historical circumstance. Augustine reported that a proverb became popular in North Africa: "If there is no rain, tax it on the Christians."[3]

In essence, Peter declared that the best defense against unbelievers' unfounded charges was a life-style which was totally above reproach. He encouraged his Christian friends to squelch slander by conduct which was consistently good, upright, and winsome.

Peter's goal was not to force the pagan world to brag on the Christians. Rather, it was that Christians' good conduct would cause the unbelievers to see God's glory and become converted.

Some students think Peter's phrase "the day of visitation" (v. 12) referred to judgment at the end of time. Other commentators think that the reference was to actual trial experiences which the Christians in Asia Minor were facing in Roman law courts. In the context of what follows in the next verses, I prefer the latter viewpoint.

As Christians, Be Good Citizens (2:13-17)

In verses 13-17, Peter began to spell out for specific situations what he meant when he counseled his friends to "maintain good conduct among the Gentiles" (v. 12). His starting line involved civil obedience and the relationship of Christians to the state.

Be Subject to Those Who Govern (2:13-14)

Peter opened his exhortation with a Greek verb form which is an aorist imperative. The imperative mood conveyed a sense of command and urgency. The command, "Be subject" (v. 13), conveyed the idea of voluntary submission to a government which, at this point, was not attempting to put itself in God's place.

For Peter, being submissive to civil authority was a basic mark of good Christian discipleship. His viewpoint in this regard was the same as the one Paul expressed (Rom. 13:1). He also was reflecting something which Jesus said about the valid role of the state in people's affairs: " 'Render therefore to Caesar the things that are Caesar's, and to God the things that are God's' " (Matt. 22:21).

Peter's appeal for submission was related directly to Christ. Do this, he wrote, "for the Lord's sake" (v. 13). This phrase may have implied that Peter was asking his readers to relate to the civil authority quietly because Jesus had told them to do so. Again, the implication may have been that they were to do this so that they would not discredit or embarrass Christ.

Peter appealed to Christians to be loyal to the authority of the state. This authority was personified in the individuals who held high official status. Peter named two offices in this regard, those of emperor and governors (vv. 13-14). Of course, the emperor was the person of greatest rank in the Roman Empire. Not yet, we believe, had the Roman Emperors assumed the role of gods. Not yet were they demanding that loyal citizens give them homage and worship. The power of the Emperor, however, was immense and awesome. If our dating suppositions are correct, the Roman Emperor at the time of Peter's writing was Nero.

The Roman governors in the first century were officials who were appointed to maintain order and to collect taxes in the various provinces of the Empire.

Peter summarized the role of civil authority in this manner: The rulers were "sent by him [God] to punish those who do wrong and to praise those who do right" (v. 14). Peter certainly would have agreed with Paul who wrote in this regard: "For there is no authority except from God, and those that exist have been instituted by God" (Rom. 13:1).

Do Right (2:15)

Again, Peter referred to false charges that were being brought against the first-generation Christians in Asia Minor: "For it is God's will that by doing right you should put to silence the ignorance of foolish men" (v. 15).

From various other sources, we know what some of the false charges leveled against Christians may have been. For example, since Christians spoke of eating the body and drinking the blood of their Lord in observing the Lord's Supper, some opponents of the faith accused them of cannibalism. From the Book of Acts, we learn that some people accused Christians of interfering with business practices and damaging trade (Acts 19:23-27). Because Christians sometimes referred to their meetings as the *Agapē*, the Love Feast, some adversaries accused them of being grossly immoral.

Against the backdrop of such charges, Peter urged his friends to practice a high level of Christian integrity and behavior that would make their opponents seem ignorant and foolish. He encouraged the Christians to silence all slander against them by the sterling quality of their piety and the appropriate righteousness of their practice.

Live as Free People (2:16)

Verse 16 deserves to be numbered among the truly great statements on the dual nature of Christian citizenship: "Live as free men, yet without using your freedom as a pretext for evil; but live as servants of God."

Freedom had been an integral part of Jesus' call to discipleship. He said: " 'You will know the truth, and the truth will make you free. . . . So if the Son makes you free, you will be free indeed' " (John 8:32,36). During his long missionary career, Paul struggled to free the gospel from its shackles in Palestinian Judaism in order that it might be set loose to claim the larger Gentile world. Paul's Letter to the Galatians sometimes has been called his declaration of independence from Judaism.

In the early days of the church, however, the call to greater freedom was misinterpreted by some converts to be a release from all restraint. Freedom in Christ and freedom from the Jewish law was held wrongly by some believers to mean that they were given moral license to do as they pleased. They lived by the principle of anything goes. This antinomian (opposed to law) approach to freedom inevitably resulted in moral chaos and anarchy. Some of the readers of 1 Peter may have felt drawn toward this persuasion.

Peter strongly affirmed the call to freedom which is at the heart of the gospel: "Live as free men" (v. 16). In God's grace through Jesus Christ, Christians are freed from the law of sin and death. They are freed from anxious guilt over the past and hopeless dread of the future. Under grace, Christians were freed from the petty legalism which characterized first-century Jewish piety. Having just encouraged his readers to be submissive, Peter now called them to exult in their freedom in Christ.

Peter was quick to caution his friends, however, against the peril of distorting Christian freedom into moral license. He wrote: "Yet without using your freedom as a pretext for evil" (v. 16). The word translated **pretext** actually meant *cloak*. Peter did not want freedom in Christ to become a covering for underhanded behavior which really was sub-Christian. Paul reflected the same thought in his Galatian letter: "For you were called to freedom, brethren; only do not use your freedom as an opportunity for the flesh, but through love be servants of one another" (Gal. 5:13).

58

Peter proceeded to declare the fuller scope of Christian freedom. The reverse side of this coin was then—and still is—Christian bondage. Peter wrote: "Live as free men, ... but live as servants of God" (v. 16). The word translated **servants** in this verse actually meant *slaves.* Peter was indicating that no genuine freedom can be known until a person has anchored his or her life in loving submission to God's will and purpose.

Be Committed Citizens (2:17)

In the last verse of the paragraph 2:13–17, Peter summarized his citizenship commitment in four terse exhortations: "Honor all men. Love the brotherhood. Fear God. Honor the emperor" (v. 17).

For Peter, the Christian ethic was all-inclusive. Although society was stratified rigidly in that day, Peter saw God's love as including everyone. He called for the believers to have God's view of the world, which includes respect for every individual as a person: "Honor all men" (v. 17).

Peter's counsel to "love the brotherhood" (2:17) referred to life within the church. Whereas Peter asked the believers to respect all people, he urged them to love their fellow Christian brothers and sisters. The Greek verb used for **love** in this verse is a present active imperative form of *agapaō.* This verb form conveyed the idea: Keep on loving. *Agapē* was the strongest kind of love referred to in the New Testament. It was the kind of spontaneous, unmotivated love which God gives to everyone with no thought of return. Peter wanted his readers to have this kind of God-like love for one another in the family of God. Of course, this did not exclude extending determined goodwill (*agapē*) to people outside God's family.

Peter's counsel to "fear God" (v. 17) did not mean that Christians were to cower before God as defenseless pawns. The reference was not to fear in the sense of terror. The word **fear** in this context meant *to hold in awe and reverence.* The writer of Proverbs used the same word in this way: "The fear of the Lord is the beginning of knowledge" (Prov. 1:7). That is to say that giving priority to a genuine reverence for God in one's daily living is the foundation for building the good life. Such a priority also becomes the foundation for all other significant knowledge. Peter wanted his readers to have this vital sense of priority in their lives.

Peter's fourth exhortation in the series in verse 17 called on his readers to "honor the emperor." The word "honor" also was used in the first exhortation. Peter wanted his friends to give the Emperor the same kind of respect which Peter had asked them to give to all other people. Whether an individual was a prince or a pauper, each deserved the Christians' respect or honor. Note in particular that Peter did not ask the believers to reverence or worship the Emperor.

The fact that Peter wrote as he did in the paragraph 2:13-17 about submission to and honor for the Emperor has an implication concerning the date of 1 Peter. The words make us think that this letter must have been written before Nero began his bloodbath reprisals against the Christians in Rome. Also, we would do well to read Peter's comments about civil obedience in light of his own action in a situation where human authority cut across his sense of duty before God. Jewish religious leaders in Jerusalem had charged Peter and the other apostles not to teach in Jesus' name (Acts 4:17-18). Peter and the apostles did not heed this warning. They continued to preach in Jesus' name. Hailed into court and confronted with their disobedience, Peter and the apostles replied with one of the great early Christian statements of Christian conscience. The words carried overtones of a kind of civil disobedience. Peter and the apostles said: " 'We must obey God rather than men' " (Acts 5:29). Ultimate authority belongs to God. Christians' ultimate allegiance must be to him. Civil government is to be honored when it is good, just, and fair. When it is bad, unjust, and unfair, it deserves no honor. And when government goes contrary to God's demands, Christians are to obey God.

Be Diligent Workers,
Even Under Stress (2:18-20)

Next, Peter directed his citizenship concern to the area of work, to what we would call employer-employee relationships. In many respects, in the first century the work-a-day world was totally different from our world today. However, Peter affirmed some broad Christian attitudes about work which were relevant then and remain so today.

The role which slavery played in the work force of the first century must be one of the major differences between the New Testament era and our own. Slavery was accepted as an established fact with little or no question by the New Testament writers. Even Paul's Letter to Philemon, the most personal New Testament document we have in this regard, only counseled that the owner receive the runaway slave, Onesimus, as a Christian brother. Paul made no explicit request that Philemon give Onesimus his freedom. Quite obviously, no strong abolition movement developed in the wake of Jesus' ministry. Had the Christians made a frontal attack on slavery as such, their budding movement likely would have been destroyed by the Roman people's strong ire.

One reason for this possibility was the sheer size of the institution of slavery in the Roman Empire. Someone estimated that the Empire had as many as 60,000,000 slaves during the first century.[4] Slavery was an integral and important part of Rome's life. Slavery developed in the aftermath of Roman conquests and the spread of the Empire. Initially, slaves were defeated pawns of warfare who were carried captive to their conquerors' homeland. Such slaves were assigned menial tasks of hard manual labor in their new countries. The Greek word for such individuals was *douloi*. Gradually, however, slaves became more than just additional hands in the work force. Slaves worked as doctors, teachers, musicians, actors, secretaries, and stewards.

The latter group of slaves usually enjoyed a preferred status, even among slaves. Often they were live-in, domestic servants who became much-loved by the families where they served. Such slaves were called *oiketai*. Still, they were slaves, which meant that they had no legal rights. They were not allowed to marry or to vote. Children born to the slaves' common-law marriages became the owners' property. At best, a slave was little more than a most-valued work animal.

As Peter wrote to the work force of his day, his comments had to be made in the general pattern of slavery which we have described. In verse 16, Peter used the commonplace Greek word for slaves, *douloi*. In verse 18, however, he used the Greek word for house servants, *oiketai*. Thus in the latter verse, Peter addressed individuals who may have known some preferential treatment in their respective work areas; yet, they remained essentially bond slaves.

Peter encouraged the domestic slaves to be submissive to their masters (v. 18). They were to do this "with all respect." Peter knew that all slave owners were not the same. Just as some employers today are fair and understanding while others are not, so in that day some slave owners were "kind and gentle," but others were "overbearing" (v. 18).

Peter indicated that the Christian slave's duty was to be submissive and respectful to any master, whatever the master's personality bent might be. Of course, to submit to a kind master would be much easier than to submit to an overbearing one. Peter stated the commonplace understanding that no particular merit was gained in taking punishment well, if one obviously had done wrong (v. 20). His indirect appeal was for Christian slaves to do right. When a slave who had done no wrong was treated harshly by an overbearing master, the slave was not to rebel. Peter advocated that in such circumstances, the Christian slave should suffer patiently (v. 20). In so doing, the slave would win God's approval (vv. 19-20).

Follow the Example of Christ (2:21-25)

Today, the method which Peter advocated of coping with stress and injustice likely would be called a type of passive nonresistance. Peter found the supreme example of this life-style in the way Jesus dealt with pain and suffering during the Passion week.

Christ Suffered for You (2:21)

Peter evidently saw the call to suffer as an integral part of the total Christian calling. He wrote: "For to this you have been called" (v. 21). As Christians were called to experience suffering, Peter wanted them always to remember that they were passing through a valley where Christ had walked before them. Christians were called to "follow in his steps" (v. 21). The Greek word translated "steps" could mean tracks or footprints.

In verses 21-25, Peter sounded one of the great themes of later Christian devotional literature—the imitation of Christ. This phrase became famous as the title of a Christian devotional classic written by Thomas á Kempis during the first quarter of the fifteenth century (1380-1425).

Peter urged the believers to pattern their lives after the legacy left behind by the "example" (v. 21) of Christ's suffering. The Greek word translated *example (hupogrammon)* had a graphic point of reference. It appears only here in the New Testament. From other sources, however, we know that the term was used to describe a writing-copy which a teacher gave to a beginning pupil to imitate. Some authors used this word to signify the copy-head at the top of a child's exercise book which the child was to imitate while learning to write. The copy-head often included all the letters of the alphabet.

Christ Trusted God (2:22-23)

Notice carefully how Peter spelled out the example of Christ which the believers were called to imitate. Jesus committed no sin (v. 22). The Greek word for sin in this verse is *hamartian,* which meant *to miss the mark.* With his sinless life, Jesus did not miss the goal which God had marked out for him. No "guile" or deceit was found on Christ's lips (v. 22). Peter had used the word *guile* earlier in his letter (2:1) when he listed the traits which believers were to put away from their lives.

Furthermore, Peter wrote that Jesus gave a strong example of patient courage and endurance under heavy stress: "When he was reviled, he did not revile in return; when he suffered, he did not threaten; but he trusted to him who judges justly" (v. 23). Even at this point in the first century, just thirty years after Jesus' death, that he did not fight back against his Jewish and Roman accusers was a well-known fact. Peter indicated that Jesus was willing to give his life and cause to the Heavenly Father who judges justly.

Christ's Wounds Heal You (2:24)

Verse 24 is important because it reflects some of Peter's understanding of what Jesus' death on the cross meant for believers: "He himself bore our sins in his body on the tree, that we might die to sin and live to righteousness. By his wounds you have been healed."

Peter's words obviously did not elaborate a fully developed doctrine of the atonement. They pointed to some dimensions of the cross-event which any doctrine of the atonement should include. Jesus Christ went to the cross, not because of *his* sins, but because of *our* sins. The reflexive pronoun intensified the phrase: "He himself bore our sins."

The Greek word translated *bore* was a common verb used to describe bringing sacrifices to the altar in religious worship. The aorist tense in this instance carried the idea of punctiliar action, that is, action which was done once but not repeated. As the bodies of animals and birds had been brought as sin offerings in the worship rituals of Old Israel, so Jesus brought his own body to

be sacrificed for our sins. The altar was "the tree"—not a living tree, but rather pieces of wood made into a cross.

Jesus gave his life on the cross in order that those who believed in him might "die to sin" (v. 24), that is, get away from or be freed from the bondage of sin. The purpose of this emancipation was that such persons might come alive, that they might live a life of righteousness before God and with other people.

The word translated "wounds" in verse 24 was a rare Greek word which is found only in 1 Peter 2:24. It pictured bruises or bloody wounds like whelps raised by a lash. When we remember that some of Peter's readers had been slaves who likely received such stripes, his language in verse 24 is graphic and stirring. By Christ's receiving such wounds, believers had been healed of their sins and made whole again.

Christ Is Your Shepherd (2:25)

In verse 25, Peter used two striking titles for the role which Christ would fulfill in the believers' lives. Note that in the Revised Standard Version, these words are capitalized: "For you were straying like sheep, but have now returned to the Shepherd and Guardian of your souls."

Of course, the shepherd figure often was used as a biblical metaphor to indicate how God providentially cared for his people (Ps. 23; John 10:11-16,27-30). The word **Guardian** was a translation of the Greek word *episkopon,* which meant overseer or bishop. Only in verse 25 was Jesus called the guardian or bishop of our souls.

Verses 21-25 as a whole bear a noticeable similarity to the prophet Isaiah's description of the Suffering Servant (Isa. 53).

Jesus had identified with the Servant concept of the Messiah during his lifetime. (See Luke 4:16-27.) The passage 1 Peter 2:21-25 shows how the early church began to see more clearly that Jesus completely fulfilled the servant role as the promised Messiah. Thus Peter challenged his Christian friends in Asia Minor to follow the most noble literary picture we have of how God acted when he came to earth.

Several concluding observations can be made about 1 Peter 2:11-25. Peter clearly sounded the call to responsible citizenship. His ethical stance essentially was positive. Christians were to silence their opposition by the positive good of their daily living, not by a coldly negative life-style. His positive approach to life was a call to freedom, but never was this liberty to become moral lawlessness.

Furthermore, Peter thought that every facet of life should be touched by one's Christian faith. Even the world of work should be influenced by one's commitment to Christ. Although Peter did not make a frontal attack on slavery, he did sound some of the chords which ultimately caused the Christian movement to become one of the deciding influences which brought about abolition. He affirmed the dignity of honest toil. He called for Christians to demonstrate that they were not disgruntled rebels. In his appeal for Christian courage and patience even in suffering, he helped lay the foundation for transforming and redeeming the whole messy business of buying and selling human beings.

Lessons for Life from 1 Peter 2:11-25

The Christian view of human nature is not dualistic, but it recognizes fully the dueling conflict which exists in each of us.— This says that the Christian faith does not advocate a separate, independent order of evil as opposed to a separate, independent order of good. In the Bible, God created all things both physical and spiritual; and all that God made was good—even "very good" (Gen. 1:31). Evil is real, but only in a parasitic way. This is to say that evil can exist only because good exists. Good, not evil, is eternal. But the Bible also recognizes that good and evil oppose one another in people's inner beings in a state of perpetual duel. Today, we need to hear Peter's appeal to his friends for a life-style which was totally above reproach.

The call to Christian discipleship is a summons to freedom and liberty which does not result in political anarchy or moral license.—Christians should be loyal citizens of their nations. But they hold a deeper, transcendent loyalty to God through Christ. Living this dual role, Christians can be ardent patriots and conscientious objectors in differing citizenship situations.

The Christian faith calls on believers to perform worship and work as to the Lord.—The Bible does not make a neat separation between the sacred and the secular in terms of life or vocation. All of life is a gift from God and should be viewed as being sacred. Christ gave believers an example in his worship and his work. We should seek to follow faithfully "in his steps" (2:21).

1. J. B. Lightfoot, *The Apostolic Fathers* (Macmillan and Co., Ltd., 1912), pp. 505-06.
2. *Ibid.*
3. Quoted by Nathaniel M. Williams, *An American Commentary on the New Testament* (Philadelphia: The American Publication Society, 1890), 6:31.
4. William Barclay, *The Letters of James and Peter* (Philadelphia: The Westminster Press, 1976), p. 247.

Personal Learning Activities

1. First Peter 2:11 marks a shift in the letter. What had gone before was theological in nature; what followed was ＿＿＿＿＿ in nature. (Choose the correct answer from the list.)
   (1) Ethical   (3) Theoretical
   (2) Doctrinal   (4) Biblical
2. Peter used two words to characterize his readers as Christians living in a hostile environment. From the list, select the proper responses.
   (1) Pilgrims   (3) Aliens
   (2) Soldiers   (4) Exiles
3. First-century Christians seldom were charged as wrongdoers. True＿＿＿ False＿＿＿
4. Peter challenged his readers to silence the ignorance of foolish people by (choose the correct answer from the list):
   ＿＿(1) Out-arguing them   ＿＿(3) Doing right
   ＿＿(2) Fighting them   ＿＿(4) Agreeing with them
5. **To live in true freedom** means *to do as you please.* True＿＿ False＿＿
6. Why did Peter not attack slavery head-on?

Answers: 1. (1); 2. (3), (4); 3. False; 4. (3); 5. False; 6. Because the Romans would crush any emancipation movement.

Our Christian Practice Begins at Home

1 Peter 3:1-12

Set me as a seal upon your heart,
as a seal upon your arm;
for love is strong as death,
jealousy is cruel as the grave.
Its flashes are flashes of fire,
a most vehement flame.

Many waters cannot quench love,
neither can floods drown it.
If a man offered for love
all the wealth of his house,
it would be utterly scorned.

—Song of Solomon 8:6-7

America's ambassador to Japan a few years ago was Douglas MacArthur II. Previously, he had served as counsel of the State Department under former Secretary of State John Foster Dulles. Like Dulles, MacArthur was a hard worker.

Once when Dulles telephoned the MacArthur home asking for Doug, Mrs. MacArthur mistook him for an aide and snapped irately: "MacArthur is where he always is—weekdays, Saturdays, Sundays, and nights—in *that office!*"

Within minutes MacArthur got a telephone order from Dulles: "Go home at once, boy. Your home front is crumbling!"

This quiet humor about "a crumbling home front" becomes serious in light of many of the signs of the time about American family life. We are not in some smoothly pocketed eddy when we come to consider the theme of our Christian practice beginning at home. We are in the mainstream of current issues where the winds are fierce and the waves are high.

When I was in Athens, Greece, on an overseas preaching mission, our party was staying at one of the suburban hotels near the beautiful Aegean beach. Early one morning, I stopped at a newsstand to see if I could find a morning paper in English. As I was paying for the paper, I saw in a prominent place several issues of a major American magazine. The bright red cover was eye-catching. So was the large headline: SPECIAL ISSUE: THE AMERICAN FAMILY. Immediately below this, my eye caught the lead article title: "Is the Family Obsolete?"

What about the possibility of the family's being obsolete? *Is the family becoming obsolete in our generation?* The magazine was discussing not a death *in* the family but a death *of* the family. Not personal grief, but the end of an era was being considered. The magazine articles were discussing the possibility that the institution would fold.

Inevitably in this age of disenchantment and attack on what sometimes is called "the establishment," the family ultimately has felt the chilling winds of criticism and despair. Various spokesmen have said that God is dead, that the church is dying, that the state is decaying. Now, some have declared that the family is becoming obsolete.

Any discussion of a complete Christian life-style should include some counsel on the vital area of the family. Peter turned his attention to this concern in 1 Peter 3:1-12.

Peter's Counsel for Wives (3:1-6)

The New Testament contains three major passages which deal rather fully with relationships within marriage and the family. Two of these are found in Paul's writings (Eph. 5:21 to 6:4; Col 3:18-21). (Actually, the words directed to slaves and masters were part of the household code. Slaves were viewed as members of households.) The other passage is 1 Peter 3:1-12 which we consider in this chapter. All three passages well could be studied together to note their similarities and their differences.

As Peter had counseled the servants to be submissive to their masters (2:18), now he counseled wives to be submissive to their husbands (3:1). His word "likewise," or in like manner, referred to the beginning of his paragraph on the relationship of servants to masters. If that discussion had been number one, the next area in sequence would be number two.

The cultural gap is vast and wide between the decade of the 60's in the first century and our contemporary era. One of the points where this divergence can be seen clearly is the role and status of women. To be sure, genuine joy and love in marriage must have been known by some couples in the ancient world—witness the romantic love stories of Jacob and Rachel, Ruth and Boaz in the Old Testament. Many good men in the Greco-Roman world no doubt loved their wives dearly. But by and large, women's status and role at this time was meager and lowly.

Under Jewish law, a wife was considered to be one of her husband's possessions. She might be a prized possession, but she still was a possession. The Tenth Commandment declared: " 'You shall not covet your neighbor's house; you shall not covet your neighbor's wife, or his manservant, or his maidservant, or his ox, or his ass, or anything that is your neighbor's' " (Ex. 20:17, my italics). Even as a prized possession, with such a mind-set a wife often was regarded as nothing more than a piece of property—a thing.

In Greek civilization, that a woman's place clearly was in the home was well-accepted. A wife was to remain indoors and be obedient to her husband. The Greeks were too polished to say crudely that a woman's place was to keep house and bear children, but this was much the sentiment which they conveyed. Under Roman law, a woman absolutely had no rights. She was regarded as a child. With the Latin legal phrase patria potestas, the Romans indicated that a woman was under the absolute power of her father. This even included the power of life or death. When she married, this autocratic rule passed to her husband. Women who broke out of this mold many times became loose and immoral.

Although Peter's counsel may seem a bit removed from the world of the sexes in the 1980's, his word about a marriage ethic was considerably higher than the accepted mores of his day. For example, although he gave more advice to wives (vv. 1-6) than to husbands (v. 7), he *did* give some pointed counsel to husbands. Thus he recognized the mutual, reciprocal responsibilities which spouses shared in Christian marriage. He also declared that wives were "joint heirs of the grace of life" (v. 7), elevating women to a place of equality with men in Christian marriage. Such thinking was quite advanced and progressive for Peter's day.

Redemptive Behavior (3:1-2)

Peter counseled wives to "be submissive" (v. 1) to their husbands. As I have indicated, the word "submissive" is the same word that Peter had used in telling servants how to relate to their masters (2:18) and citizens how to relate to the state (2:13).

Submission was not a spineless groveling in the dust and a forced denial of basic selfhood. Peter did not suggest that in marriage, the wife ceased to be a person. Rather, he advocated what has been called a "voluntary selflessness" which was based on the death of pride and the desire to serve. It was not a submission out of fear but a submission in love, the kind of perfect love which casts out fear (1 John 4:18).

We also should note that the wives' submission was to be only to their *own* husbands. The Greek word *idiois* in 3:1 strengthens the idea of the marriage relationship's exclusiveness. In other words, Peter instructed wives *not* to be submissive to the husbands of other women.

In the larger context of this passage, Peter addressed Christian wives who were married to non-Christian husbands (v. 1). The situation of one spouse's becoming a believer when the other was not, often created problems for the early Christians. This dilemma still causes strain in marriages.

Peter gave a reason for wives' being submissive to their husbands: "so that some, though they do not obey the word, may be won without a word by the behavior of their wives" (v. 1). He used a form of *logos*, word, twice in this verse. In the first occurrence, *logos* was used in the technical sense of the Word of God, the gospel. The second instance referred to words spoken by other people, and, probably in particular, words spoken by Christian wives. Peter urged the believing wives to win their unbelieving husbands to faith in Jesus Christ not by nagging, but by pious living. Note the significant role that Peter called on the wives to assume.

The word translated "behavior" in verses 1 and 2 is the same

Greek word which Peter had used earlier as he encouraged his readers to maintain good conduct among their non-Christian peers (2:12). At this point, Peter spelled out such conduct or behavior as being "reverent and chaste" (3:2).

The Revised Standard Version's translation of verse 2 differs from some other translations. In the Greek, for example, no word occurs for "coupled" (v. 2, KJV). In this context, the word "reverent" is the most appropriate translation of the Greek word. Peter appealed for behavior among the Christian wives which reverenced God, not for conduct which was based on fear of their husbands.

The word **chaste** (v. 2) meant pure. As such, it was a word which was used by both Christian and non-Christian religious groups. Originally, the word referred to an attribute of deity. However, it came to refer to moral uprightness and integrity on the part of individual worshipers. Peter appealed for Christian wives to be clean, pure, and above reproach in their total lifestyle.

As he continued, Peter became more specific about the coiffures and fashions of Christian wives: "Let not yours be the outward adorning with braiding of hair, decoration of gold, and wearing of fine clothing" (v. 3). The Roman ladies of that period wore no hats. Their accepted high fashion included elaborate hairstyles. Jeweled combs, gold headbands, ribbons, and other showy jewelry were considered good by fashion-conscious Roman women. Also, women of means often made lavish expenditures for their wearing apparel.

Peter reacted negatively to Christian women's showy approach to style and beauty. Of course, he did not encourage carelessness in dress and personal cosmetic care. However, he did advocate that Christian wives should be discreet and modest in their mode of dress and their use of beauty aids. You would be interested to note that the term translated **outward adorning** in verse 3 came from the Greek word *kosmos*. The older meaning of this word was *ornament*, but the more common reference of the word was to the world as an orderly whole. The Greek word *kosmos* gives us our English word *cosmetic*.

Peter looked on lavish outward adornment as a kind of ornamentation or worldliness which Christian wives would do well to avoid. Were Peter living today, he probably would have some problems accepting the cosmetic artistry of many American women.

The Hidden Person of the Heart (3:3-4)

Peter's appeal was for another kind of adornment, not made with sterling silver but with sterling character: "But let it be the hidden person of the heart with the imperishable jewel of a gentle and quiet spirit, which in God's sight is very precious" (v. 4). The phrase "hidden person of the heart" referred to the real self, or the real person, deep within the heart and soul. Peter's insight reminds me of these lines by the Scottish poet, Robert Burns:

> Nae treasures nor pleasures
> Could make us happy lang;
> The heart ay's the part ay
> That makes us right or wrong.[1]

The jewelry which Peter recommended was not the showy rings, ribbons, and armlets which many women of his day wore. Beautiful as such finery might be, it was not a lasting beauty. Precious metals can become corroded, and precious jewels can be shattered and/or stolen.

Peter urged Christian wives to adorn themselves with the imperishable jewel of a gentle and quiet spirit. For Peter, Christian beauty was a matter of modesty, not makeup. Peter wrote that such traits were "precious" in God's sight. The term translated **precious** was an old Greek word which carried the idea of value. It was used only two other times in the New Testament.

A Godly Example (3:5-6)

Peter's example of proper behavior for first-century Christian wives was Sarah, wife of the Old Testament patriarch, Abraham. As a part of her faith in God (v. 5), Sarah was obedient and submissive to her husband, Abraham. On one occasion, she referred to her husband as "My lord" (Gen. 18:12, KJV). Peter urged Christian wives in his day to become daughters of Sarah by doing right and letting nothing terrify them (v. 6).

The last part of verse 6 echoed one of the Old Testament Proverbs (3:25). Apparently, Peter's concern was that some non-Christian husbands would try to scare or threaten their wives out of the wives' Christian faith. Peter urged these Christian women to hold fast to their faith, even under extreme provocation from their husbands.

An illustration of Peter's overall counsel to Christian wives may be found in one of the literary classics from Christian history. Augustine, the stalwart churchman from North Africa and Milan,

wrote in his *Confessions* of the influence which his Christian mother, Monica, had over his pagan father. Augustine described his mother's successful endeavor to win her husband to belief in God: "preaching Thee unto him by her conversation; by which Thou ornamentedst her, making her reverently amiable, and admirable unto her husband."[2]

Peter's Counsel for Husbands (3:7)

The Permanency of Marriage (3:7a)
Most appropriately, Peter counseled men to be good Christian husbands. As we have said, the fact that Peter recognized mutual responsibility in Christian marriage was a most progressive step for his day. Both theologically and ethically, this put Peter's grasp of the role of the sexes in marriage far ahead of first-century Greco-Roman writers.

Although Peter used only one verse to give his counsel to husbands, his brief words expressed some powerful, far-reaching ideals. The basic thought underlying Peter's counsel to wives and husbands was that all relationships in Christian marriage are mutually reciprocal. This concept that both spouses should share equally in the responsibilities of marriage was implied strongly in the first three words of verse 7: "likewise you husbands." In all probability, these words referred to Peter's phrase in 3:1: "likewise you wives."

Peter continued verse 7 with a present active participle verb form which was used as an imperative. The word was an old verb which referred to domestic association. This reference was the only time this word was used in the New Testament. A literal translation of this line would read something like this: Likewise you husbands keep on living in the house with your wives. In our day, when trial separations and easy divorces are common, this exhortation alone would be strong advice from Peter.

The Need for Understanding (3:7b)
But verse 7 contains much more. Peter wrote: Live at home "considerately" with your wives. The words translated **considerately** literally meant *according to knowledge.* Peter seemed to understand clearly that stability and permanence in marriage depended on more than just romantic feelings and pretty words. He saw that

75

a maturing marriage must be undergirded by clear thinking, good judgment, and kind understanding. In other words, Peter would say that a good marriage needs both heart power and mind power. A Christian husband should live at home with his wife using the best intelligence he possesses to love her and care for her.

The Demand for Respect (3:7c)
As he continued, Peter's counsel became stronger: "Bestowing honor on the woman as the weaker sex." Earlier in his letter, Peter used the word "honor" in this way: "*Honor* all men. Love the brotherhood. Fear God. *Honor* the emperor" (2:17, my italics). Christian husbands were to relate to their wives with the same courteous respect which they would give to the ruling king or to people in general. Peter's words were not a call for male chauvinism but for male chivalry.

For us to realize how startling Peter's counsel in this regard really was, is difficult. In the ancient world, common courtesy and chivalrous action to women was almost unknown. Peter clearly indicated that unthoughtful behavior by a husband toward his wife is not Christian.

We also should note that Peter's reference to women as "the weaker sex" was not a matter of chauvinistic condescension. Peter certainly did not mean that women were or are inferior to men. The word translated **sex** at this point is not the term which ordinarily was used for referring to sexuality. The most common usage of this word meant *vessel* or *utensil*. In the idiom of our day, we best could say that generally, women are weaker *physically*. Peter's intended meaning quite simply was that as a general rule, women are not as strong physically as men. He was not saying that women are weaker mentally than men. And from his next statement we know that Peter believed that spiritually, men and women are equals.

Let us paraphrase what is implied by what Peter has written in verse 7 to this point: As I wrote to your wives, so in like manner, I would address you husbands. I would remind all of you that each spouse shares in the responsibility of nurturing a maturing marriage. Each of you husbands should keep on living in the house with your wife, using your best intelligence to love her and care for her. Give honor and respect to your wife with all courtesy and kindness, because physically she is the weaker person in your marriage.

Heirs Together (3:7*d*)

Peter added still another reason why Christian husbands should relate to their wives in love, courtesy, and kindness: "Since you are joint heirs of the grace of life" (v. 7), relate to your wives in this way. The term "joint heirs" is a late compound word in the Greek language which has been found by archaeologists in an inscription at Ephesus and in many of the later papyri. This word occurs in the New Testament in only three other references (Rom. 8:17; Eph. 3:6; Heb 11:9).

Thus, in verse 7 Peter used a word which two other New Testament writers had used to describe the basic dimensions of God's relationship to his people. The concept of mutuality and equality is dominant in all three of these references. From its primarily theological setting, Peter applied this word to Christian marriage. The analogy implied an exalted view of marriage. As God had made Gentiles joint-heirs of his grace through Jesus Christ (Eph 3:6), so husbands and wives in Christian marriage were coequals of the grace of life. Whatever submission Peter had envisioned for Christian marriage definitely was a submission of equals.

We also should note Peter's phrase, "the grace of life" (v. 7). Peter used the word **life** in the Johannine sense of *eternal life* (John 1:4; 3:16). He saw Christian husbands and wives as joint heirs through God's grace in the "imperishable" inheritance (1:4) which is kept in heaven for men *and* women. In Peter's mind, heaven would have no place for either male chauvinism or female feminism. Both sexes would be coequal joint heirs through God's grace in Christ.

One clause remains from the significant verse 3:7 in Peter's letter: "in order that your prayers may not be hindered" (v. 7). In these words, Peter declared that a poor relationship between a Christian husband and his wife contributed directly to a poor relationship between the individual believer and God. Strained personal ties in marriage hinder a couple's prayer life. Behavior which isolates a Christian husband from his wife also can isolate him from God.

A further inference can be drawn from the final clause of verse 7. Peter seemed to think that Christian couples would pray together often. Today, many of us likely would be embarrassed to admit how little in-depth praying we do together in our homes as husbands and wives.

Peter's Counsel for Both Spouses, and All Other Christians (3:8-12)

Basic Christian Virtues (3:8-9)

Peter introduced the paragraph 3:8-12 with an adverb: "finally, all of you" (v. 8). The word "finally" (*to telos* in Greek) did not refer to the end of the letter. Instead, it referred to the end of a section of the letter which probably began at 2:13.

In the immediate context, since Peter had addressed wives and husbands in the immediately preceding verses, we might conclude that the phrase "all of you" in verse 8 referred to husbands and wives together. As we will see, the exhortations which follow certainly could be applied to the roles of both spouses in marriages.

More likely, however, the phrase "all of you" gathered into one group the whole of Christian society—citizens, servants, wives, husbands, and all other persons who were first-century believers in Asia Minor. This inclusive summary of Christian virtues applied not only to interpersonal relationships within marriage but also to interpersonal contact throughout the church and community.

Peter enumerated six characteristics of an authentic Christian life-style. These traits make up the heart of Christian attitude and behavior in terms of how we live with one another, both at home and in the church.

Response to One Another (3:8).—Peter expressed the first five notes in his ethical appeal like this: "Have unity of spirit, sympathy, love of the brethren, a tender heart and a humble mind" (v. 8). We should note that leading this list was a call for oneness and harmony among the believers. In a real sense, each of the other traits mentioned were attitudes or mind-sets which could contribute to a spirit of unity among God's people. The prince of this world, the devil, likely never is pleased more than when he successfully sows seeds of friction, hostility, and division in a home or in a church family. The Greek word translated **unity of spirit** in this verse literally meant *likeminded* or *of the same mind*.

The next four virtues are related closely. Obviously, Peter thought that each of these traits could make a vital contribution to unity and oneness in the family and in the church. The word

sympathy is a direct transliteration from the compound Greek word *sun* (with) *pathos* (suffering). A sympathetic person suffers with, or feels with, those whom he or she loves. "Love of the brethren" was just one word in the Greek, *philadelphoi*. As you know, the name of one of our major American cities is a direct descendant from this word. Philadelphia is the city of brotherly love. We should add that "brethren" is used generically in verse 8, so that brothers and sisters—both sexes—are included. Incidentally, this was a well-known Greek word in the first century; it is used only here in the New Testament.

The next two traits are set forth by words which are considered late words in the Greek language. The word translated "a tender heart" is found in the Apocrypha and in the medical writings of Hippocrates. It is used only twice, however, in the New Testament—in this verse and in Paul's Letter to the Ephesians: "Be kind to one another, *tenderhearted*, forgiving one another, as God in Christ forgave you" (Eph. 4:32, my italics).

"Tenderhearted" is the opposite of hardhearted. (See Ezek. 3:9; Prov. 28:14; Mark 3:5.) In light of our discussion in 1 Peter 2, to note that Jesus used the phrase *hardness of heart* when speaking to the Pharisees about marriage and divorce is interesting: "For your *hardness of heart* Moses allowed you to divorce your wives, but from the beginning it was not so" (Matt. 19:8, my italics). When tenderheartedness gives way to hardheartedness, life at home and in the church faces grave perils.

The phrase "a humble mind" also is only one word in Greek. Peter's reference in verse 8 is the only use of this word in the New Testament. Having a humble mind meant that a person was aware of his or her creatureliness before God. With Christian humility, a person never should look on a marriage partner, or any other person, as being inferior.

Response to Evil (3:9).—Peter spelled out the sixth characteristic of an authentic Christian life-style more fully. He wrote: "Do not return evil for evil or reviling for reviling; but on the contrary bless, for to this you have been called, that you may obtain a blessing" (v. 9). The Christian task of overcoming evil with good had been affirmed both in Jesus' teachings and in Paul's writings.

We may conclude that the New Testament message in general ruled out the get-even attitude of life. Ray Summers made a precise comment on this dimension of Christian living: "It is a part of the proverbial vocabulary of Christianity that: to return evil for good is animal-like; to return evil for evil is human-like; to return good for evil is God-like."[3]

Peter was in the mainstream of New Testament thought as he urged his Christian friends in Asia Minor not to live by a dog-eat-dog ethic, but to demonstrate a commitment to overcoming evil with good. Such a pattern of life would make them known as the children of God. Peter believed that living in this way enabled a person to be a blessing and to receive a blessing (v. 9).

Achieving the Good Life (3:10-12)

Peter concluded the perceptive passage 3:8-12 with a beautiful quotation from Psalm 34. Note that in the Revised Standard Version, these verses are translated in poetic form. The positive thrust of the passage is exciting.

What is the secret of finding the good life? Residential community planners often advertize that the good life can be discovered by buying a home in their real estate development. Does finding the good life depend primarily on where we live, or on how we live?

Peter and the psalmist declared that achieving the good life is more a matter of attitude or spirit than it is a matter of geography. They counseled persons who loved life and wanted to see good days to follow these moral guidelines:

1. Keep your conversation clean.
2. Keep your words honest.
3. Shun all evil.
4. Do right.
5. Earnestly seek peace.

Lou Holtz, head football coach at the University of Arkansas, has only one rule to guide his players in their general conduct. With a keen directness which is a mark of Lou's "one liners," his crisp counsel has only two words: "Do right!" The coach might not know it, but his rule reflects the wisdom of Peter's New Testament letter and one of the magnificent Old Testament psalms.

Read again the five guidelines listed above, and think how they can apply to life at home, in the church, in the community, and everywhere.

In conclusion, Peter quoted the psalmist further. The eyes and ears of the Lord are open and responsive to "the righteous" (v. 12). The implication is that righteous persons are those who live by the stated moral guidelines. In contrast to this, "the face of the Lord is against those that do evil" (v. 12). To use the concept of the Lord's face was to refer to the divine presence. Peter and the psalmist saw God relating to his people either with mercy or with judgment, depending on their dominant life-style.

Peter's exhortation to do right (v. 11) prepared for his transition to the next section of his letter. This, in turn, becomes the basis for the next chapter in this book.

Lessons for Life from 1 Peter 3:1-12

For Christian men and women, beauty is a matter of character more than cosmetics.—Outward adornment and mod fashions too quickly can become hollow shells incapable of sustaining life and love; they cannot replace Christian commitment and loyalty. Glamorous glitter alone will not enable a marriage to mature.

A basic foundation for Christian marriage must include the following attitudes: essential equality, reciprocal responsibility, happy honesty, genuine forgiveness, and mutual respect and love.—Marriage is a dynamic arena which offers almost unlimited opportunity to demonstrate one's Christian faith.

Whatever submission Peter envisioned for Christian marriage, it was a submission of equals.—Peter wrote of husbands and wives as being "joint heirs of the grace of life" before God (3:7). Joint heirs were always coequals. In Peter's mind, heaven would have no place for male chauvinism or female feminism. In this vital area of life, husbands and wives would do well to practice a little bit of heaven on earth!

The good life is not measured by money, things, status, or power but by quality of redeemed character.—The good life involves incorporating God's principles for living, striving to meet his high demands which accompany his gift of salvation. Life at its best has a sound spiritual base.

---

1. "Epistle to Davie, a Brother Poet," *The Complete Poetical Works of Robert Burns* (New York: Houghton Mifflin Company, 1897), p. 32.

2. *The Confessions of Augustine*, Book IX.

3. Ray Summers, *The Broadman Bible Commentary* (Nashville: Broadman Press, 1972), 12:161.

Personal Learning Activities

1. When Peter admonished Christian wives to be submissive to their husbands, he indicated that men are superior to woman. True_____ False_____

2. Peter's reason for instructing that Christian wives be submissive to their husbands was (choose the correct answer from the list):
   _____(1) To insure order in the home
   _____(2) So that wives might win unchristian husbands by the wives' behavior
   _____(3) To keep women in their places

3. Peter indicated that the proper adornment for Christian wives was _____. (Select the proper response from the list.)
   (1) Gold and silver jewelry   (3) Cosmetics
   (2) Costly clothes   (4) The hidden person of the heart

4. Peter was not as concerned to instruct Christian husbands as he had been to instruct Christian wives. True_____ False_____

5. Peter mentioned five basic Christian virtues. List three.

Answers: False; 2. (2); 3. (4); 4. False; 5. Unity of spirit, sympathy, love of the brethren, a tender heart, and an humble mind.

6

Our Christian Privilege: Standing for the Right

1 Peter 3:13-22

Since then Your Majesty and your lordships desire a simple reply, I will answer without horns and without teeth. Unless I am convicted by Scripture and plain reason—I do not accept the authority of popes and councils, for they have contradicted each other—my conscience is captive to the Word of God. I cannot and I will not recant anything, for to go against conscience is neither right nor safe. [Here I stand, I cannot do otherwise.] God help me. Amen[1]

—Martin Luther
Diet of Worms,
April 17, 1521

In the fall of 1965, my family and I moved to our present pastorate. We are now well beyond fifteen years of service with this congregation, which happens to be the longest tenure for a pastor in the 127-year history of our church. Relationships of love and ministry are deep.

A longer pastorate provides a full storehouse of memories—many happy, some sad, several funny, and still others unusual. One of my unforgettable experiences came in the early years. In fact, it was in 1966 during our first summer at the church. Twelve years had passed since the monumental 1954 Supreme Court decision regarding desegregation in the public schools. For all practical purposes, however, my new hometown was still a segregated city.

In early discussions with the pulpit committee, I had asked about race relations and public schools in the city. A member of the committee, who was also superintendent of schools, answered: "We are one step ahead of having a lawsuit, and one step behind having a riot. It's that tight."

I remembered those words the summer afternoon that a first-grade teacher came by the study to talk with me about her work plans for that fall. This teacher was considered to be one of the best first-grade teachers in the city school system.

My teacher friend began her personal remarks to me with deliberate care. She told me of her love for teaching and her many years of classroom experience. She indicated that she was nearing retirement age. She was hoping that her last few years of teaching would be remembered as her best.

Becoming more serious, my friend told me that the superintendent of schools had contacted all teachers requesting volunteers to cross the color line when the fall term opened, becoming the first stage of faculty-level racial integration in our city. She said that she had a growing conviction that this was something which she should volunteer to do.

She added: "I have mentioned this to some of my friends, and they think I'm crazy. They tell me I'm too old to try this sort of thing. I'm a rather well person, but I really don't know that I would be able physically to cope with this new kind of teaching situation. . . . Some of my friends have said that I will be ostracized by the white community if I do this. Others have said that I would lose half of my friends by doing this. . . . I want to volunteer, but then I am afraid. . . . What do you think I should do?"

As we were searching for an answer, my friend became quite reflective. She told me that as a teenage girl, she had felt God's call to become a missionary. She would have volunteered to go to Africa had this sense of call been pursued. This was not the case, however, in her unfolding life.

"But now," she added, "I have the feeling that God may be giving me a second opportunity to do something that would have real mission dimensions to it. The need is obvious. It seems so right for me to help meet it."

My teacher friend volunteered to be in the first faculty-level school integration in our city. She lost some of her friends. She was ostracized by some people in the white community. The physical and emotional strain of her new post was taxing. But she made it!

I never will forget the sparkle in her eyes as she told me shortly after Christmas of that first year: "I have my class where we would have been if I had stayed in my former school!"

With the help of this Christian teacher, plus many like her, our city turned a corner in the pilgrimage toward better understanding and respect between the races. My friend was living proof that standing for the right sometimes can be difficult, but always it is redemptive.

The Beatitude of Persecution (3:13-15)

Suffering for the Right (3:13-14a)

Earlier in our study, we noted that 1 Peter is a part of the persecution literature in the New Testament. The title of this book indicates that Peter's letter was a message to encourage the Christians who were experiencing hard times. Although we do not know the exact nature of this persecution, it obviously was more than some imagined menace. Peter later wrote of the ominous threat as a "fiery ordeal" (4:12).

At the point 3:13 in his letter, Peter picked up the persecution theme in earnest. He wrote: "Now who is there to harm you if you are zealous for what is right?"

Although stated in the form of a question, Peter's words were a positive appeal for Christians to stand for the right. His language reflected the phraseology of Isaiah (50:9), which is quite obvious in the Septuagint translation.

The word translated *zealous* in verse 13 is the same Greek word which gives us the title *Zealot*. As you may know, the Zealots were a first-century Jewish political party. They were passionate patriots who had pledged to liberate their country from Roman rule. Peter was encouraging his Christian friends to love the right, or the good, with the same kind of intensity with which ardent patriots loved their country. He pointed out that an aura of invincibility surrounded those who unflinchingly were committed to the right.

In verse 14, Peter wrote words which echo one of Jesus' Beatitudes. In the eighth Beatitude, Jesus said: " 'Blessed are those who are persecuted for righteousness' sake, for theirs is the kingdom of heaven' " (Matt. 5:10). Note the similarity to Peter's words: "But even if you do suffer for righteousness' sake, you will be blessed" (v. 14).

As previously indicated, we do not know the exact nature of the persecution which the Christians were facing. Quite obviously, however, the duress was related to their Christian faith and conduct. In verse 14, Peter referred to suffering "for righteousness' sake." In a later verse, he referred to those who reviled the Christians' "good behavior in Christ" (v. 16). In still later verses, Peter wrote of the stress like this: "as you share Christ's sufferings" (4:13), and "if one suffers as a Christian" (4:16).

The root idea behind the word "righteousness" was straightness. These believers were living straight lives in the name of Christ. In a real sense, the non-Christian world was always as Paul described it to the Philippian Christians: "a crooked and perverse generation" (Phil. 2:15). To demonstrate a Christian life-style in such a world meant that believers often went against the grain of accepted cultural patterns of their day. Such lives almost inevitably incur some hostility and opposition. Like Jesus had said, Peter declared that suffering for this reason brought its own inherent joy.

Facing Opposition Without Fear (3:14b-15a)
In the situation in which his readers suffered "for righteousness' sake," Peter urged them to muster a real Christian courage: "Have no fear of them, nor be troubled, but in your hearts reverence Christ as Lord" (vv. 14-15). In the original language, the last part of verse 14 contained an interesting bit of alliteration. Peter literally wrote: Fear not their fear. Or we might say: Fear not their threats. He did not want his Christian friends to be troubled or disturbed by the taunts, jeers, and acts of reprisal which they were facing. He saw that one way to summon such valor was to "reverence Christ as Lord" (v. 15a). The Greek verb translated **reverence** in verse 15 literally meant *set apart*. A literal translation of the statement is: Set apart in your heart, Christ as Lord.

A Christian Defense (3:15b)
In verse 15 Peter gave one of the great apologetic statements in the New Testament: "Always be prepared to make a defense to any one who calls you to account for the hope that is in you, yet do it with gentleness and reverence."

Anyone who has worked in a scouting program is familiar with

the exhortation, "Be prepared!" Peter began the key sentence in verse 15 with an intensive word added to this kind of declaration: "*Always* be prepared." A literal translation of what follows would read like this: Always be prepared to give an apology.

The word *apology* (*apologian* in Greek) in verse 15 does not mean an excuse or an apology in the sense of saying, I'm sorry. Instead of this meaning, the word was used in the sense of giving a defense for what you believe.

Peter urged his friends to be ready to give a reasoned, intelligent explanation of their faith to anyone who might ask about what Christians believed and practiced. More specifically, Peter wrote: "Be prepared to make a defense . . . for the hope that is in you" (v. 15). As a rule, the word *hope* was used to refer to the eschaton, the end of the age and Christ's return. In verse 15, however, Peter likely used the word as a synonym for the whole warp and woof of Christian belief—past, present, and future.

From his first-century setting, Peter knew that a critical need existed for Christians in the fledgling churches to be able to give a convincing verbal defense of their faith. Although we are now the heirs of almost two thousand years of Christian history, a similar need still exists.

Obviously, Peter knew that some people would defend their religion in such a manner that their words would hurt the faith rather than help it. Persons who declare their faith in Christ with dogmatic arrogance tend to repulse the people they are trying to win. Consequently, Peter added some qualifying conditions to set forth the manner in which our faith in Christ is defended best.

In the first place, Peter urged his friends to state their case for Christianity with "gentleness." A modern ad man might paraphrase the statement like this: Their defense was to be tough, but, oh, so gentle! The Greek word used is sometimes translated *meekness*. This word could be used to describe a wild horse which had been broken to the bit and saddle. The animal's strength had not been lessened. The raw, untamed nature, however, now was disciplined and brought under control so that the horse's strength could be used most constructively.

In the second place, Peter called on his friends to defend their faith with "reverence." Many tenets about God in Christ we assuredly can hold, but in truth we never can declare that we know all about God. We can know much about God with great assurance; yet, we never can get all of God into any box of our own making. Even when we defend our faith with confidence, we never should be cocky. A reverent humility should temper our strongest affirmations.

Our Best Defense: Genuine Christian Conduct (3:16-17)

As a third qualifying condition, Peter urged his friends to undergird their verbal defense of the faith with an exemplary Christian life-style. He wrote: "And keep your conscience clear, so that, when you are abused, those who revile your good behavior in Christ may be put to shame" (v. 16).

Inconsistency between one's words and one's deeds never has been the hallmark of great Christian witnessing. Peter urged his readers to keep their practice of the faith in line with their profession of the faith.

The first verb form in verse 16 is a present tense, active participle, which carried durative action. Peter was indicating: Keep on keeping your conscience clear. He knew that a Christian's best protection is "good behavior in Christ." The phrase "in Christ" is reminiscent of Paul's writings. For both Paul and Peter, it was synonymous with being a Christian. Peter realized that in the final court of appeal, the most compelling defense of the faith is the argument of an authentic Christian life.

In verse 17, Peter affirmed what we might call a kind of common-sense Christian ethic: "For it is better to suffer for doing right, if that should be God's will, than for doing wrong." J. B. Phillips has caught the mood of this verse well in his translation: "If it is the will of God that you should suffer it is really better to suffer unjustly than because you have deserved it."

To consider the will of God in relationship to any human suffering opens a vast area for study and contemplation. The entire message of the Book of Job, for example, deals with this major theological-ethical issue. Peter just touched the edge of this concern in verse 17. We should note that his language did not make a direct correlation between God's will and human pain. In fact, the mood of the Greek verb in this clause specifically posed suffering as a possibility, not as a certainty.

I think Peter would have agreed with the conclusion that God's will may allow, or permit, suffering; but God is not a direct causative force in all suffering. If suffering came within God's permissive will, Peter rightly believed that for the Christian person to suffer for doing right rather than for doing wrong was far better.

Christ Is Our Example in Suffering (3:18-20)

Christ's Redemptive Death (3:18)
To mention the possibility of persons suffering who had done no wrong reminded Peter of Jesus' Passion. In verse 18, Peter wrote one of the great New Testament affirmations of the atoning nature of Christ's death on the cross. His language was terse, but the truth was compelling: "For Christ also died for sins once for all, the righteous for the unrighteous, that he might bring us to God, being put to death in the flesh but made alive in the spirit" (v. 18).

You will note that the Revised Standard Version footnotes the word "died," indicating that some ancient manuscripts read "suffered." In the Greek language, the two words are quite similar: died (*apethanen*) and suffered (*epathen*). In this context, little or no difference seems to be made in the meaning no matter which word is used.

Earlier, Peter pointed to Christ's example as a model for how Christians should react to suffering with patient endurance (2:21-25). This theme was sounded again in verse 18. Again, the imagery is reminiscent of Isaiah's description of the Suffering Servant (Isa. 53).

In writing that Christ died "for sins," Peter used language which was associated with the Old Testament sacrificial system (Lev. 5:7; 6:30). This also was New Testament language. Paul wrote to the Corinthian Christians: "Christ died for our sins in accordance with the scriptures" (1 Cor. 15:3). He wrote to the Galatian Christians: "Christ . . . gave himself for our sins" (Gal. 1:3-4). John wrote of Jesus: "He is the expiation for our sins" (1 John 2:2). The author of the Book of Hebrews described the high priest's function as that of offering sacrifice for the people's sins (5:1-3); then, he identified Jesus as the perfect High Priest (5:7-10).

Thus, in whatever way we finally interpret the mystery of the cross, Peter and other New Testament writers declared that Jesus' death was the sacrifice which atones for mankind's sins. He did not die for his sins, but for our sins.

In verse 18, Peter also affirmed the unique dimension of Christ's suffering death which made it a nonrepeating event. Using a word which the writer of Hebrews used (9:26-27), Peter declared that Jesus' death was "once for all." This word is far different from the storybook phrase, "once upon a time." The Greeks had a word which carried this meaning, but that is not the word which Peter used. The word Peter used implied that Christ's death on the cross was once for all *time*. His sacrifice also was once for all *sin* and once for all *people*.

The next phrase in verse 18, "the righteous for the unrighteous," literally reads: just for unjust. The original language included no articles. The reference, of course, was to the vicarious nature of Christ's death on the cross. He took our place, suffering in our behalf. He who was sinless took our place as sinners to restore our lost relationship with God.

Peter's next phrase focused on the restored relationship to God: "that he might bring us to God." William Barclay described two graphic uses of the Greek word which is translated "bring" in this verse.[2]

One use of the word bring was primarily Jewish in background. In the Old Testament, this word described the bringing to God of men who were to be priests. For example, God said to Moses: "You shall bring Aaron and his sons to the door of the tent of meeting" (Ex. 29:4). The tent of meeting was the place among the Exodus pilgrims where Moses had his most direct encounters with God before the tabernacle was built.

In the larger context of Jewish worship, we could add that only Aaron and his sons were to come to the door of the tent. Other persons who were not priests were to keep their distance.

The rigidly stratified approach to God in Jewish worship became more apparent after the Temple was built. The Temple building plan allowed worshipers to move toward God only in set and limited ways, dependent on who they were. Non-Jewish people could enter only the outer Court of the Gentiles. All Jewish people could enter the next Court of the Women, but only Jewish men could proceed into the Court of the Israelites. Only those who were priests could go into the Court of the Priests. Finally, only the high priest could enter the holy of holies.

In sharp contrast to the Jewish-Temple manner of approaching God, Jesus' death on the cross cut through all such religious protocol. The way was opened for all people to be brought to God. This new openness was symbolized in Matthew's Gospel by the report that the curtain or veil of the temple was "torn in two, from top to bottom" (27:51) when Jesus died.

Another use of the word translated bring in verse 18 stemmed from its Greek background. The noun form of this verb meant the right of access or the result of the bringing in.

In a king's court during Peter's era, one of the officials was called "the introducer." In the Greek language, this title was a transliteration of a form of the word meaning bring. The introducer, or bringer, was a giver of access. His function included deciding who would be admitted to the king's presence and who would be refused. With this graphic word picture, Peter declared that by Christ's death on the cross, he became the One who gives people access to God.

In the last phrases of verse 18, Peter affirmed the paradox whereby death and life were present in the cross event: "being put to death in the flesh but made alive in the spirit." Peter saw Jesus' death on the cross as being real. Jesus did not merely faint or fall into a coma. He physically died.

Peter also saw the spirit of resurrection at work in Christ's death on Friday even before the decisive resurrection on the first day of the next week. In other words, Peter saw Jesus being alive in the spirit before Jesus experienced what we know as the bodily resurrection. Pursuing this idea briefly, Peter introduced the most difficult passage in his letter.

Christ's Preaching to Imprisoned Spirits (3:19-20)

In fact, verses 19-20 are numbered among the most controversial passages in the entire New Testament. Peter wrote: "in which he [Christ] went and preached to the spirits in prison, who formerly did not obey, when God's patience waited in the days of Noah, during the building of the ark, in which a few, that is, eight persons, were saved through water" (vv. 19-20). These lines, along with 4:6, have given rise to many varying interpretations. They influenced the early church fathers to include this sentence in the Apostles' Creed: "He descended into Hell."[3] Roman Catholic churchmen have sought to find in these verses some biblical support for a doctrine of purgatory.

A. T. Robertson stated frankly that verses 19-20 have caused more controversy than anything else in the epistle. Martin Luther admitted that he did not know what Peter meant in these verses. Whatever interpretation we finally decide to affirm, our position should be a classic instance in which we give a defense for the hope which is in us, as we have just indicated, with gentleness and reverence (3:15).

Obviously, to present a detailed account of how verses 19-20 have been interpreted in the history of Christian thought is beyond the scope of this study. A brief summary in this regard, however, should include at least the following viewpoints:

1. Jesus went to the realm of the dead—Sheol or Hades—between his death and resurrection. This was a part of his suffering for the sins of all people.

2. Jesus made this journey to proclaim his lordship over the dead. His goal was to obtain release for the righteous people who had died prior to the cross.

3. Jesus went to the realm of the dead to validate what God had been saying throughout history. God's redemptive work now had been accomplished in Christ's death on the cross. For those who

had refused to respond to the truth of God which had been available to them, Jesus as the crucified Lord confirmed their damnation.

4. Jesus went to preach repentance and salvation, offering the disobedient spirits either a first or a second chance at being saved.

5. The passage has nothing at all to do with Christ's descent into hell. Instead, it refers to his being present through his eternal spirit at the actual time of the disobedience. For example, this would mean that Christ, through his eternal spirit, was present in the days of Noah. Every beat of Noah's hammer while he was building the ark was a call from Christ's eternal spirit for that generation to repent and believe God.

6. By a textual error, these verses refer to Enoch, not to Jesus. An apocryphal story in the Book of Enoch mentions Enoch's giving a proclamation of doom to the fallen, imprisoned angels (Enoch 6:4). Of course, the Book of Enoch is not recognized by the canon of either the Old Testament or the New Testament.

The unresolved questions which these verses bring to mind are many. For example, during his hours in the tomb from the time of burial until resurrection dawn, where did Jesus' spirit go? When did he go? What did he preach to whomever he went? Why was the preaching addressed only to disobedient spirits "in the days of Noah"? In what sense were eight persons "saved through water" in Noah's time? Even after careful study of this passage, many of us still will have more questions than we have answers.

Whatever viewpoint you most nearly endorse in this regard, some salient truths can be affirmed from verses 19-20 which transcend any specific position. For example, these verses clearly state that Jesus' death was not make-believe. If Christ descended into Hades, then his death was no sham.

Incidentally, hades is a more exact term than hell. In Jewish thought **hades,** or **sheol,** was the shadowy realm of the dead. **Hell,** or **gehenna,** was the place of punishment. It was so named from the Valley of Hinnom just outside the walls of Jerusalem where the city's refuse was burned. The New Testament does not say that Jesus descended into hell; that is, gehenna. The implication is strong in verses 19-20, however, that Jesus descended into hades—the realm of the dead.

Second, if the preceding thought be true, then Christ's triumph over all times and places is universal. God's message of grace in Christ reaches out to touch all mankind so that no person is excluded from the scope of God's love and concern.

From Peter's reference to the disobedient spirits in the days of Noah, he commented about the ark which Noah built (v. 20). During the great flood, the ark became the instrument of salvation for Noah and his family—a total of eight persons (Gen. 7:6-13). The ark was actually a symbol of Noah's obedience to God which was in sharp contrast to his peers' disobedience.

From our point of view, for Peter to say that Noah and his family were saved by the ark rather than by the waters of the flood would have been more exact. Except for Noah and his family, the flood waters destroyed everyone else.

Evidently with his next illustration in mind, Peter wrote of Noah and his family as being "saved through water" (v. 20). As Ray Summers rightly concludes, "The only way the water can be spoken of as saving them is in its bearing up the ark in which they had taken refuge."[4] From this line of thought, Peter made an interesting comment about Christian baptism.

Christian Baptism: Symbol of the Resurrection (3:21-22)

From his reference to Noah, the ark, and the floodwaters, Peter moved quickly to a significant comment about Christian baptism. He wrote: "Baptism, which corresponds to this, now saves you, not as a removal of dirt from the body but as an appeal to God for a clear conscience, through the resurrection of Jesus Christ" (v. 21). The main thought of this verse reads like this: "Baptism . . . saves you . . . through the resurrection of Jesus."

In verse 21, Peter used the Greek word *antitupon*, which occurs only one other time in the New Testament (Heb. 9:24). From this Greek term, we get our English word *antitype*, which means *that which is prefigured or represented by the type.* The Revised Standard Version reads: "which corresponds to."

Peter was saying that Noah's deliverance by the floodwaters was an antitype of the Christian believer's deliverance which is symbolized in baptism. Similar examples from biblical thought would indicate that the Old Testament Passover Lamb was an antitype of Jesus in the New Testament. The Exodus from Egypt was an antitype of the entire cross-event.

Peter clearly spelled out his understanding that Christian baptism was far more than just a rite of cleansing. It was not a bath to remove dirt from the body. Instead of this, Peter saw baptism as a symbolic act—"an appeal to God for a clear conscience."

Such an appeal implies that baptism was done publicly in contrast to being done privately. In being baptized, the new Christian was making an open pledge, or vow, of consecration to God. This public proclamation indicated that the believer had made a thorough inquiry, had repented of his or her sins, and had turned to God for salvation through Christ's resurrection. The pledge or appeal of a clear or good conscience made baptism the symbol of an inward change of heart.

Peter stated clearly that baptism was associated directly with

Jesus' resurrection. Paul made the same correlation in his Letter to the Romans (6:3-4). Such identification with Christ in his death and resurrection meant that the believer died to an old life and arose to live a new life. Later Christian practice in the second century made this understanding of baptism quite graphic. The baptismal candidates took off their old clothes and entered the water from one side of the pool. They were immersed, and then they went out on the other side of the pool and put on new clothing.

Further, we should note that in no way can baptismal regeneration be read into verse 21. For Peter, baptism was not a sacramental, saving rite. Baptism had no efficacy apart from Christ's resurrection. Baptism was a symbolic picture of Christ's resurrection and also a dramatic portrayal of the individual believer's redemption.

In verse 22, Peter affirmed Jesus' ascension: "who has gone into heaven and is at the right hand of God, with angels, authorities, and powers subject to him" (v. 22).

Although Jesus suffered and died in the cause of standing for the right, death did not defeat him. He arose from the dead, and he experiences a glorious destiny. The Suffering Servant has become the reigning Lord. He is at God's right hand, holding a place of honor and recognition. All powers—good and bad—ultimately are subject to him. He is the triumphant Christ. Peter was assuring his friends that although believers in Christ may suffer great difficulties, they will triumph finally just as Christ has triumphed. Who among us follows in his train?

Lessons for Life from 1 Peter 3:13-22

Christians should not expect to be praised always for doing what is right.—A pecking order exists in human society which sometimes means that people will pick (or peck) on those who try to do right. At school, in the plant, and in the community at large, some people are embarrassed when their peers try to go straight. Peter echoed Jesus in affirming that those who are persecuted for righteousness' sake will be blessed.

Christians need to be able to give a verbal defense of their faith.—In the day-to-day world of conflicting opinions and values, Christians need to be able to say what they believe and why they believe it. These statements need to be made in the right spirit—with gentleness and reverence. A right answer can be given with such a wrong spirit that it appears rudely repulsive rather than compellingly attractive.

Christ's death on the cross was God's attempt to offer atonement to all people everywhere.—Peter described Jesus' experience on the cross as a "once for all" (3:18) kind of event. Christ's death on the cross was once for all time. His sacrifice was also once for all sin, and it was once for all people.

---

1. Quoted by Roland H. Bainton, *Here I Stand* (New York: Abingdon Press, 1950), p. 185. Bainton noted: "The earliest printed version added the words: 'Here I stand, I cannot do otherwise.' The words, though not recorded on the spot, may nevertheless be genuine."

2. William Barclay, *The Letters of James and Peter* (Philadelphia: The Westminster Press, 1958), p. 276.

3. *Ibid.*, p. 280.

4. See Ray Summers, *The Broadman Bible Commentary* (Nashville: Broadman Press, 1972), 12:163-64.

Personal Learning Activities

1. Peter wrote that Christians were to be prepared to make a defense of the hope that was in them with _____ and _____. (Choose the correct answers from the list.)

   (1) Gentleness   (3) Aggressiveness
   (2) Dogmatism   (4) Reverence

2. Peter maintained that the Christian's best defense was (select the proper response from the list):

   ___(1) The Bible   ___(3) Silence
   ___(2) Good behavior in Christ ___(4) Secrecy

3. Which interpretation of the statement, "He [Christ] went and preached to the spirits in prison" (1 Pet. 3:19), do you prefer? Why?

4. In Jewish thought, hades or sheol was (choose the correct answer from the list):

   ___(1) Heaven   (3) The shadowy realm of the dead
   ___(2) Paradise   (4) Hell

5. Peter wrote that baptism is a symbolic picture of Christ's resurrection and of the believer's redemption. True___ False___

Answers: 1. (1), (4); 2. (2); 3. Your answers; 4. (3); 5. True.

7

Remember Who You Are and Live Like It
1 Peter 4:1-6

MIST: I don't believe the sleepers in this house
  Know where they are.
SMOKE: They've been here long enough
To push the woods back from around the house
And part them in the middle with a path.
MIST: And still I doubt if they know where they are.
And I begin to fear they never will.
. . . .
SMOKE: If the day ever comes when they know who
They are, they may know better where they are.
But who they are is too much to believe—
Either for them or the onlooking world.[1]

—Robert Frost
"A Cabin in the Clearing"

Likely you will recall some of the incidents from two famous children's books written by Lewis Carroll: *Alice's Adventures in Wonderland* (1865) and its sequel *Through the Looking Glass* (1872). These two nineteenth-century volumes are said to have been quoted more often than any other literary works except the Bible and Shakespeare's writings.

In chapter 2 of *Through the Looking Glass*, Alice was walking in the garden of live flowers when suddenly she was met by the Red Queen. Walking together to the top of a little hill, the queen and the young girl saw the countryside stretched out before them to the distant horizon.

For Alice, the interlacing brooks and hedgerows made this panorama look like a large chess board. At first, she thought that the squares were empty. Then she began to see various chess pieces moving about the vast area. Alice wanted to join the game, even as a Pawn.

The Red Queen said that Alice might have her wish. She would become a Pawn, the White Queen's Pawn. When Alice had moved forward to the eighth square, then she might become a queen herself!

Before leaving Alice on her own to move across the precarious chess field, the Red Queen said: " 'Speak in French when you can't think of the English for a thing—turn out your toes as you walk—and remember who you are!' "[2]

As a young boy, I was not introduced to Alice's adventures. I discovered these fanciful tales later as an English major in college. I was quite familiar, however, with the words, "Remember who you are!" As a preschooler leaving the house to go to a friend's birthday party, I can remember my mother saying, "John, remember who you are."

Growing up during the 1930's and 1940's, I always went to church with my family. Father, mother, two sons, and one daughter went together. Fortunately, early in 1941 we bought a new family car. A two-door Ford sedan, this car was to last us throughout the duration of World War II. Sitting in the back seat of that car with my brother and sister en route to Sunday School and church on Sunday morning, often I have seen and heard my mother look back on her brood and quietly say, "I hope you will remember who you are!"

So it was for me. Off to some teenage party, off to college, off to out-of-state graduate school, I often received this counsel: "John, remember who you are!" Initially, these words conveyed to me that I was a vital part of a real family. I was not to behave in any way that would shame or disgrace my family. Later, as we all became Christians, my mother's counsel reminded me that I was part of Christ and his church. My behavior never should bring shame or disgrace to my Savior or to my church.

Thus, as a McClanahan and as a Christian, often I was told: "Remember who you are!" Now in mid-adulthood, I recall this as good counsel. Note how these words seem to catch the mood of this next section in Peter's letter. Peter wanted his friends to remember who they were, and to live like it!

Arm Yourselves for the Fray (4:1-2)

Ready for Suffering (4:1)

Peter opened the section 4:1-6 with a transitional clause which referred to his thought in 3:18. He wrote: "Since therefore Christ suffered in the flesh, arm yourselves with the same thoughts, for whoever has suffered in the flesh has ceased from sin" (4:1).

Peter's point of departure in verse 2 should be clear. Since Jesus experienced physical suffering, those who believe in him should expect to undergo the same treatment. Note the footnote in the Revised Standard Version which indicates that some manuscripts read: "Christ suffered in the flesh *for us*," or *"for you.*" With or without this addition, the meaning is the same. Again Peter was affirming the vicarious and redemptive nature of Christ's agony on the cross. (See 3:18.)

Peter proceeded to use a martial word in urging the Christians to get ready for the foreboding times which were approaching. The phrase "arm yourselves" actually translates a term from military language. It was used to command soldiers to take up their equipment for battle. The word is found only in verse 1 in the New Testament.

Peter's exhortation, however, was not a call to arms in the usual sense of that word. Instead of their using weapons, Peter urged his friends to arm themselves "with the same thought" (4:1) which Jesus had. We might express his idea like this: Arm yourselves with the mind-set of Christ. Again, Peter presented Jesus as an example for his readers; they were to follow in his steps.

The last part of verse 1 seems to point to a direct relationship between physical suffering and exemption from sin. Peter was not indicating what some later churchmen held, that martyrdom was an atonement for sin which was like a second baptism that washed the soul clean. He was contending that the level of Christian commitment that brings one to the point of being willing to suffer for his or her faith tends to make a person better able to resist temptation and sin.

Living by God's Will (4:2)

The commitment that Peter called for would produce a marvelous result: "so as to live for the rest of the time in the flesh no longer by human passions but by the will of God" (v. 2).

The Greek verb translated **live** appears only in verse 2 in the

New Testament. It carried a durative idea and meant *to spend a life.* Peter urged his friends to live in a certain way for the remainder of their earthly lives.

The manner of life which Peter recommended presupposed the *dueling* nature of human existence. As noted earlier, nowhere in the Bible do we find human nature described in terms of full-blown *dualism.* The emphasis of biblical thought was on the unity of persons.

The Greeks were dualists. They saw a person as a soul entombed in a body. The main goal of life was to free the soul from the dregs of the body. In contrast to this, Hebrew-Christian writers saw a person as a body-soul. The highest aim of life was to glorify God both in the body and in the soul, that is, with one's whole being.

Hebrew-Christian writers recognized a kind of divisive split in human nature. Rather than this being a *dualistic* view of people, these writers saw a *dueling* aspect in human nature. They pointed to a continuing struggle for dominance which takes place in people's inner beings.

Peter reflected the dueling concept of human nature as he urged his friends no longer to allow their lives to be dominated by human passions. In contrast to such a secular life-style, Peter called on his friends to let God's will be the determining influence in their lives. In the next verses, Peter described in more detail what he meant by the phrase "to live . . . by human passions."

Enough Is Enough! (4:3-5)

Putting Gentile Living Behind (4:3)

For Peter, living by human passions was playing copycat to a Gentile life-style. Such a manner of life was incompatible with faith in Christ. Peter expressed himself in strong, forthright words: "Let the time that is past suffice for doing what the Gentiles like to do, living in licentiousness, passions, drunkenness, revels, carousing, and lawless idolatry" (v. 3).

A popular song some years ago was entitled "Doing What Comes Naturally." For Peter, Paul, and other New Testament writers, a person never would reach any degree of Christian morality by doing what came naturally. The natural person always was an unredeemed person. By nature, people were and are sinners, not saints. Doing what the Gentiles liked to do was doing what came naturally for unregenerate people.

Peter declared that his Christian friends should let the time that was past suffice for the kind of behavior he described. The word **suffice** in this verse meant *enough*. Any kind of behavior like this was too much. But by all means, these persons had done enough of this sort of thing in the past. As first-generation Christians, they were to remember who they were! Their future lives were to be free from all such sub-Christian practices.

Peter named six specific sins which the Christians no longer were to follow. His exhortation lets us know of the radical change of life-style which was demanded of persons who were converted to faith in Christ from the rank paganism of the first-century Gentile world.

Peter's list of vices in verse 3 was an apt description of a life-style which was flagrantly immoral and godless. The Greek word translated **licentiousness** (RSV) meant *lasciviousness* (KJV) or *unbridled lustful excesses*. The word referred to what today we might call rank sensuality or raw sex. It pictured a permissive, loose morality at its worst.

The word translated **passions** is the same word found in verse 2. This Greek term meant *lust* (KJV). The word referred to sexual desire, not as a beautiful, God-ordained gift but as a misused, degrading appetite.

The word translated **drunkenness** literally meant *winebibbing*. It was an old compound word composed of the noun for *wine* and the verb *to bubble* up or over. It is found only in verse 3 in the New Testament. Obviously, the word referred to an excessive use of fermented grape juice. If Peter opposed the excessive use of naturally fermented wine in the first century, how much more would he oppose the use of more potent, distilled, alcoholic beverages today? In the light of Peter's strong admonition against drunkenness, today's Christians are challenged to take a firm stand against beverage alcohol.

The next two words referred to similar immoral excesses. The word translated "revels" (RSV) was used to describe prolonged drinking-fests which often occurred with the pagan religious celebrations. It carried the idea of what we might call orgies. The word translated "carousing" referred to drinking parties which were more social in nature. It was an old word for drinking bouts. It is found nowhere else in the New Testament. We should note that in the six specific sins which these new Christians were to shun, three were related to the misuse of beverage alcohol. Again, this fact has strong, unmistakable implications for today's Christians in a society in which drinking beverage alcohol is of epidemic proportions.

The last vice listed in verse 3 is translated "lawless idolatry" (RSV). We would be more exact to say lawless idolatries, because the Greek word is plural. In fact, the Greek noun forms cited in this verse for all six sins are plurals.

From the Jewish-Christian viewpoint, all idolatries were unlawful or "abominable" (KJV). But particularly offensive to the Christian conscience were the false worship rites which included excessive drinking and immoral sensuality. Peter declared that a valid Christian life-style must be devoid of all such practices.

Abused for Right Living (4:4-5)

Note that Peter began in verse 4 with the third person personal pronoun "they." He wrote: "They are surprised that you do not now join them in the same wild profligacy, and they abuse you; but they will give account to him who is ready to judge the living and the dead" (vv. 4-5).

To whom did the word "they" (v. 4) refer? In all probability, the reference was to persons who previously had been friends and associates of the believers whom Peter was addressing. Peter almost seemed to mean: What you were makes them surprised at what you are now!

Some of those persons who formerly had been a part of the wild debaucheries no longer would come to the parties. The Greek verb translated **join** (v. 4) is graphic. It is a present active participle form of a compound verb which meant to run together as a crowd or a mob. Literally, Peter meant: They are surprised that you do not keep on running with the same old crowd.

The new Christians' former drinking buddies and carousing partners did not understand their behavioral change. Reflecting a morality that was no higher than the pecking order in a chicken yard, the used-to-be friends began to ridicule and abuse the Christians for their changed life-styles.

The situation reflected in verse 4 should give us some insight into the kind of persecution that Peter's readers were experiencing. At this point, the persecution probably was more personal than political. Rather than being a vendetta organized by Rome, more likely it was—at least in part—the petty viciousness of broken friendships. Such individual attacks involved pain and hurt; but likely, life and limb not yet were being taken.

Peter assured the Christians that their former friends would be held accountable for their (the former friends') hostile actions. Like all other persons they, too, would be judged. Peter did not make clear whether the Judge in mind was God or Christ. Evidently, he could think of God (1:17) and Christ (1:13) in this role.

Judgment Is Coming (4:6)

The Gospel Preached to the Dead (4:6*a*)
Whether God the Father, God the Son, or both filled the role of Judge, Peter was convinced that an ultimate judgment for each person was a definite part of the final end of things. As we shall see in chapter 8 of this book, he also believed that this final end was near.

Verse 6 in the overall passage 4:1-6 must be understood in light of the two ideas of the impending end and an ultimate judgment. Peter wrote: "For this is why the gospel was preached even to the dead, that though judged in the flesh like men, they might live in the spirit like God."

Verse 6 has been interpreted in various ways. As noted in textbook chapter 6, some students link verse 6 with 1 Peter 3:18-20. They view it in light of the possibility that Christ descended into hell or hades. They read into this verse the idea that the gospel was preached to those who had lived and died before Christ's time, or that the gospel offered a second chance for those who died as unbelievers in any era.

Strong reasons exist, however, for disassociating verse 6 from 1 Peter 3:18-20. Linguistically, the vocabulary is not the same. The words for preaching in the two passages are different: *proclaim* (*ekēruzen*) (3:19) and *evangelize* (*euēggelisthē*) (4:6). In the earlier reference, the persons involved were called "spirits in prison" (3:19). In the later reference, the persons involved were called "the dead" (4:6).

We are on safer ground to interpret verse 6 in its immediate context. What went immediately before, and what came immediately after? Immediately before, in verse 5, Peter wrote of the divine judgment which was coming on "the living and the dead."

The contrast clearly was between people who were alive and people who were dead. In verse 6, when Peter referred to the gospel being preached "even to the dead," he used the same word for "dead" as he had used in verse 5. Thus, he was writing of persons who were physically dead, not just spiritually dead in trespasses and sins.

A Pressing Question (4:6b)

Immediately after verse 6, Peter referred to the *eschaton*—the end of time (v. 7). He thought of the end of all things as being near—"at hand."

Today, we often wonder about the spiritual status of people who die without having heard about Jesus Christ. To Christians who were living in the first century, however, a much more pressing problem was phrased like this: What about those persons who became Christians but died before the Lord Jesus returned to claim his own? Was their faith in vain?

Peter answered the question with a firm No! Such Christians' faith was not in vain. We might paraphrase Peter's answer to the question like this: Even for those who have died as believers in Christ, this is why the gospel was preached to them. Although death brought a certain judgment to them as it did to all people, as Christians they lived again in the spirit like God. Though physically dead, as believers they still will share in the triumphant victory of Christ's second coming.

Thus, Peter concluded that judgment was coming for all persons, whether they were alive or dead. Those who believed in Christ could be assured, however, that after judgment they would know eternal life with God. Believers would receive this inheritance whether they were alive or dead physically when the end of all things occurred.

Lessons for Life from 1 Peter 4:1-6

Conflict is inevitable when a person seriously seeks to live a Christian life-style.—At times, this conflict will assume the proportion of actual warfare. In his letter, Peter used a military term to summon Christians to the martial task of Christian discipleship (4:1). We echo such biblical imagery when we sing the gospel song, "Onward, Christian Soldiers." Christians do not use force to win converts, but they are called to stand forcefully against the entrenched power of evil in the world.

Authentic Christian living will require that believers say a firm, resolute No to certain kinds of behavior.—High on Peter's list of sins in this category were sexual immoralities and drunken carousing. Whether then or now, any kind of behavior like this must be regarded as being totally unchristian.

Final judgment is a part of our total Christian faith.—Everyone will be held accountable before God. Believers in Christ may be assured that after judgment, they will have eternal life in the spirit like God and with God.

---

1. Edward Connery Lathen, ed., *The Poetry of Robert Frost* (New York: Holt, Rinehart, and Winston, 1969), pp. 413-15.

2. Lewis Carroll, *Alice in Wonderland* and *Through the Looking Glass* (Kingsport, TN.: Grosset & Dunlap, Pub., 1946), p. 175.

Personal Learning Activities

1. Peter admonished his readers to arm themselves with (choose the correct answer from the list):
   ____(1) Swords   ____(3) Clubs
   ____(2) Christ's mind-set ____(4) Courage
2. Peter contended that physical suffering issued in exemption from sin. True_____ False_____
3. Peter challenged his readers to live by _____. (Select the proper response from the list.)
   (1) Civil law   (3) God's will
   (2) The law of Moses   (4) The golden rule
4. In light of what Peter wrote about drunkenness, what should be the Christian's stance toward beverage alcohol in our society?
5. When Peter referred to the gospel's being preached to the dead, he meant that (select the proper reponse from the list):
   (1) Christ had descended into hades
   (2) The gospel had been preached to people while they lived, and now they were dead
   (3) Those who died as unbelievers received a second chance to respond to Christ

Answers:
1. (2); 2. False; 3. (3); 4. Your answer; 5. (2).

106

---------- **8** ----------

"Don't Dally," It's Later Than You Think

1 Peter 4:7-19

"When I go and prepare a place for you, I will come again and will take you to myself, that where I am you may be also."

"We must work the works of him who sent me, while it is day; night comes, when no one can work."

"Watch therefore, for you know neither the day nor the hour."

Jesus
John 14:3; 9:4
Matthew 25:13

" 'There was a fearful black cloud riven by darting tongues of flame, which then dissolved into long plumes of fire. We could hear the shrieks of women, the screams of children. Most were convinced that this must be the end of the world.' "[1] Pliny the Younger wrote these words in a letter addressed to the Roman historian, Tacitus, giving an eyewitness account of the eruption of Mount Vesuvius in AD 79. This is the most famous volcanic explosion in history. The blast buried the Roman towns of Pompeii and Herculaneum, located just a few miles south of Naples.

At least 2,000 persons were killed by the lava, steam, and hot ash which spewed from the crater. Included in this number was the Roman admiral and historian, Pliny the Elder, who died while trying to help refugees flee from the site of the eruption. Pliny the Elder was an uncle to Pliny the Younger. The latter Pliny also served from around AD 111-13 as governor of the Roman province of Bithynia in Asia Minor. Of course, this was one of the provinces addressed by the New Testament letter of 1 Peter. You will recall that in chapter 1 of this textbook, the information was given that Pliny the Younger referred to the Christians living in his province in letters to the Roman Emperor Trajan. These letters are the earliest descriptive accounts of the life and customs of Christians written by a nonbeliever that we possess.

The tragic loss of life in Pompeii and Herculaneum was heightened by the fact that such personal disaster might have been avoided. Residents in those cities had received ominous warnings that something in the general terrain was not right. In fact, a series of earthquakes and tremors had alarmed people in the neighborhood of Vesuvius for 16 years, or from AD 63.

Although some families probably moved out of the area, most residents remained where they were. Vesuvius was known to be an old volcanic crater, but it had been dormant for hundreds of years. Because most people had no memory of an eruption, they assumed that another one never would occur.

But on August 24, AD 79, how wrong they were! Mount Vesuvius "blew its top," and over 2,000 persons lost their lives. For 16 years they had been warned. But because of unconcerned dallying, they did nothing.

While this textbook was being written, an awesome volcanic eruption again became headline news. On Sunday morning, May 18, 1980, Mount St. Helens in Washington State erupted with a stupendous explosion of trapped gases. Geologists estimated the blast to be 500 times the force of the atomic bomb dropped on Hiroshima. They considered it to be on about the same order of magnitude as the eruption of Vesuvius in AD 79.

The entire mountaintop was blown away in a single burst. Clouds of hot ash and pulverized rock belched twelve miles into the sky. Gigantic mud slides of melted snow and ash rumbled down the slopes. Millions of towering trees were knocked down, leaving the great forest area looking like a giant had been playing pickup sticks.

Total damages from the eruption were estimated in staggering, multimillion-dollar figures. A number of persons were killed and many others were missing.

Mount St. Helens' eruption was the first volcanic activity in the Cascade Mountain Range of the western United States since 1914. As in the days of Pompeii, residents in this general area had been forewarned that a volcanic eruption might be brewing. As early as March 27 before that fateful Sunday in May, some natural signs pointed to the possibility of an eruption. Although the area was sparsely populated, most of the people continued life as usual.

When the warning signs became more ominous, some people moved out, but others refused to budge. As in the days of Pompeii and Vesuvius, some people on Mount St. Helens needlessly lost their lives. Either from carelessness or stubbornness, they delayed responding to the alarm.

First Peter 4:7-19 expresses the author's urgency to his friends in Asia Minor. He was not writing about an approaching volcanic eruption; he was writing about a coming event of ultimate significance. He believed that the end of time for all mankind was drawing near. Peter wanted his friends to be ready for this impending event.

The Imminence of the Eschaton (4:7)

As Peter drew near to the end of his letter, he wrote of another terminal end which he believed was drawing near. He wrote bluntly: "The end of all things is at hand" (v. 7).

Peter's language was clear. By "the end of all things," he meant the end of the present world order. Primarily, two Greek words were used in the New Testament to refer to the consummation of the ages—*eschaton* and *telos*. In verse 7, Peter used the latter word.

The verb form translated "is at hand" is the same word Matthew used when he recorded John the Baptist's preaching relative to the impending approach of the kingdom of heaven. John proclaimed to the people of his day: " 'Repent, for the kingdom of heaven is at hand' " (Matt. 3:2).

Peter picked up the word *ēggiken* and applied it to Jesus' expected return or second advent. James also used the same word and applied it specifically to Jesus' second coming: "You also be patient. Establish your hearts, for the coming of the Lord is at hand" (Jas. 5:8). Like many other New Testament writers, Peter expected Christ's second coming, and the consequent end of time, to be in the near future.

Living with the End of All Things in View
(4:7-11)

A Creative Tension (4:7)

Because Peter expected the end of time at any moment, a real sense of urgency pervaded his counsel to his friends in the provinces. He believed that people who realized the nearness of Jesus' return would commit themselves zealously to more dedicated Christian living. Peter would not have been pleased with a casual, dallying response to his deep concern.

Peter gave what we might call an interim ethic for the crisis time. Expecting Jesus' imminent return did not weaken the ethical demand in Peter's understanding of the Christian faith. His eschatology heightened his ethical commitment. "In a word, this sense of living 'between the times,' on what is at once the edge of the old and the edge of the new, gives life a unique tone and temper, and makes the chief end of man the glory (or manifestation) of God."[2]

Note carefully the paragraphing in this part of Peter's letter as seen in the Revised Standard Version. The initial statement in verse 7 stands as the topical sentence for the entire paragraph. Everything in the paragraph that follows is related to the initial affirmation: "The end of all things is at hand" (v. 7). The transitional word "therefore" appears only once in this paragraph. It well might be repeated several times, however, because all the statements which follow are made in light of the expected nearness of the *eschaton*.

The Need for Prayer (4:7)

Peter wrote: "The end of all things is at hand; therefore keep sane and sober for your prayers" (v. 7). J. B. Phillips translated the second half of this verse: "Therefore be calm, self-controlled men of prayer."

The first verb form in verse 7 is an imperative which conveyed a mood of urgency. We could paraphrase it: In light of the expected end of time, Be calm!—Or Keep cool. The actual Greek verb meant being of a sound mind. The Revised Standard Version's **Keep sane** means: *Be sensible* or *reasonable*.

The second word in this key exhortation is translated **sober**. In this context, the word had nothing to do with abstaining from the use of alcoholic beverages. Neither did it refer to being excessively dour and/or serious. Instead, the word meant *to be self-controlled*.

We should note that Peter used these two words with specific reference to the prayers which the early Christians would pray. Even though they expected all things to end soon, their prayers were to be fervent but not foolish. They were to pray with sincerity, sensibility, and self-control.

The Call to Maintain Christian Love (4:8)

Peter continued: "Above all hold unfailing your love for one another, since love covers a multitude of sins" (v. 8). His words made plain that being ready to rendezvous with the Lord at his second coming in no way lessened the Christians' responsibility to love their fellow human beings.

Peter's language in verse 8 again is graphic. Love still was to be the top priority for authentic Christian behavior. It was to be "above all" other concerns. The Greek word translated **unfailing** is an adjective formed from a verb stem which meant to stretch out or stretch toward. This particular word is found only in verse 8 in the New Testament.

The word "unfailing" (ektenē) pictured Christian love as being an impulse which stretched—even strained—to reach out and touch other people. This was no play-it-safe or don't-extend-yourself ethic. In fact, Peter saw Christian love as being the opposite of this approach to life. The nature of agapē love is that it stretches forth to the point of straining to express care and concern for fellow human beings.

The verb form which is translated "hold" (v. 8) is a present active participle. The present tense carried the idea of durative action. Thus Peter was indicating that such an extended love was to be not just an occasional practice among Christians. It was to be the hallmark of their lives. It was something which they were to keep on keeping on doing.

One reason for constantly extending love is that this kind of love "covers a multitude of sins" (v. 8). The phrase does not mean that love makes us blind. Love does help us to overlook many wrongs done to us. However, Peter probably meant that love forgives. When we genuinely love someone, we forgive more easily. Agapē love makes being patient easier.

The Demand to Practice Hospitality (4:9)

Peter's thought continued to be occupied by the conviction that the end of time was near. We should note that this idea did not

cause him to foster an ethic of withdrawal or escape. Instead, he encouraged his Christian friends to remain in the mainstream of life. Rather than asking the believers to become starry-eyed hermits, Peter urged them to be good, down-to-earth hosts and hostesses. He wrote: "The end of all things is at hand; therefore. . . . Practice hospitality ungrudgingly to one another" (vv. 7-9).

By hospitality, Peter was not referring to what we call social entertainment. He meant board and lodging for traveling Christians. The word translated **hospitality** in this verse is an old compound term which means *friendly to strangers.*[3] The word *stranger* included even foreigners and/or aliens.

The actual practice of gracious hospitality made possible the mission work of the early church. For all practical purposes, Christian hospitality became a type of carte blanche expense account whereby missionaries could move from one place to another. Peter called on his friends to help one another "ungrudgingly" in meeting this critical need.

William Barclay pointed out that without such hospitality, the early church could not have existed.[4] Traveling missionaries had to stay somewhere. They had no place to stay except in fellow Christians' homes. Commercial inns as such were few in number. The inns which were available were quite expensive, quite filthy, and quite immoral.

The Exhortation to Be Good Stewards (4:10-11)
Peter added one further exhortation about the kind of life-style which was demanded of Christians who would live their lives with the end of all things in view. He wrote: "The end of all things is at hand; therefore. . . . As each has received a gift, employ it for one another, as good stewards of God's varied grace: whoever speaks, as one who utters oracles of God; whoever renders service, as one who renders it by the strength which God supplies; in order that in everything God may be glorified through Jesus Christ. To him belong glory and dominion for ever and ever. Amen" (vv. 10-11).

Have you heard someone describe another person like this: He (or she) has *charisma!* People in public life—especially politicians—often are described as persons who do or do not have *charisma.* Although the word **charisma** has been much in vogue in recent years, it is not a new word. In fact, it is an old Greek term which meant *a gift of grace.* In the early church, this word referred to all spiritual graces and endowments. Peter used this word in 4:10.

Contemporary usage of the word *charisma* indicates that some persons have it and other persons do not. Note that Peter's usage was not like this. His understanding was that all Christians had *charisma*: "as each has received a gift (*charisma*)" (v. 10). Peter thought that every believer has some gift from God which can be used for God's glory and for service to other people in Christ's name.

The word **employ** in verse 10 of the Revised Standard Version translates the Greek verb *diakonountes* from **diakoneō** which means *to serve* or *to minister*. This verb stem also gives us the word *deacon*. The verb form in verse 10 is a present active participle which carries durative action. Thus Peter was urging the believers to keep on serving or ministering to one another, as the end was drawing near.

Peter wanted the believers to be "good stewards of God's varied grace" (v. 10). The word translated **steward** literally meant *house-manager*. The word translated **varied** meant *many-colored*. The gifts of God's grace are not all the same. They are as variegated as human personality. But all of God's gifts can be managed or utilized in such fashion that they will minister to other people.

Peter referred specifically to a twofold division in God's manifold gifts of grace—speaking for God and rendering service through his strength. As we might say today, Peter saw Christian proclamation and Christian ministry to be inseparably united in any complete Christian witness. Those who teach or preach should do so with a sense of conviction and responsibility that they are voicing God's truth to their hearers. Those who act out their faith in practical Christian service should do so with the awareness that they are serving in Christ's name through the strength which God supplies.

The King James Version introduces both areas of Christian witness with an "if" clause—"If any man speak, . . . if any man minister." In Greek grammar, these are both first class conditional clauses. This grammatical construction presupposes or assumes that what is mentioned is, or will become, an accomplished fact. Thus, Peter had no doubt that Christians should and would be involved in both dimensions of the total ministry.

Another word picture from verse 11 is graphic. In the phrase "by the strength which God supplies," the Greek verb translated

supplies is *chorēgei*. The initial meaning of this word was *to lead a chorus*. Quite obviously, our word *choreography* comes from this Greek stem. We do not have to use much imagination to see that Peter described our total Christian witness as a majestic symphony of sound and movement—like a mighty chorus or orchestra—with God as the conductor-director. Furthermore, the verb *chorēgeō* came to mean *to defray the cost of a chorus, to supply funds*. God will supply necessary strength.

With such graphic imagery, we should not be surprised that Peter closed the section 4:7-11 of his letter with a burst of praise. His words are something like a Hallelujah Chorus in miniature: "In order that in everything God may be glorified through Jesus Christ. To him belong glory and dominion for ever and ever. Amen" (v. 11).

Being Christian in a Non-Christian World (4:12-16)

The Ordeal of Testing (4:12)
In the paragraph 4:12-16 of his letter, Peter returned to a theme which he had sounded previously (1:6-7; 2:20-21; 3:13-17)—the awesome threat of violent persecution which his friends were facing. He wrote: "Beloved, do not be surprised at the fiery ordeal which comes upon you to prove you, as though something strange were happening to you" (v. 12).

Again, Peter addressed the believers with a term of endearment and warmth. (See 2:11.) We know from Luke's record in the book of Acts that Peter knew what suffering because of his faith in Christ meant (5:17-18,40-41; 8:1; 12:1-5). Consequently, he must have felt a deep sense of identity and empathy as he used the salutation, "Beloved."

Peter reminded his readers that they should not be "surprised"—astonished or amazed—as their life situations became increasingly difficult. He spoke of the gathering storm of hostility against the believers as "the fiery ordeal." If our early dating for this letter is correct (AD 61-63), no Christians had been burned at the stake. This would come later in the reign of the madman, Emperor Nero. Nero blamed the Christians for the great fire in Rome and argued that for them to become human incendiaries was just punishment.

At the time of Peter's writing, the fiery ordeal seemed to be only an ominous threat. Peter's words likely were more symbolic than real. The fiery ordeal would not annihilate the Christians, but it would test them. Peter's language was a reference to the process of smelting gold and silver. Earlier in his letter, he had used the same word for burning fire in a metaphor which made the smelting analogy even clearer (1:7). This word probably was derived from the reference to the smelting process in Proverbs 27:21. In smelting, the metal is not destroyed; it is purified as the dross is burned away. Peter saw his Christian friends facing this kind of difficult, yet exciting situation. He counseled them not to think that this kind of circumstance was "strange"—or unusual—for Christians.

Sharing Christ's Sufferings (4:13-14)

Verses 13-14 of chapter 4 in Peter's letter echoed the spirit and some of the wording of Jesus' eighth Beatitude in the Sermon on the Mount (Matt. 5:10-12). This was the only Beatitude which Jesus repeated twice. Evidently it was as surprising to Christians then, as it is now, that they should rejoice when they suffered. Peter encouraged his friends with these words: "But rejoice in so far as you share Christ's sufferings, that you may also rejoice and be glad when his glory is revealed. If you are reproached for the name of Christ, you are blessed, because the spirit of glory and of God rests upon you" (vv. 13-14).

In suffering because of their faith, the Christians were doing something which Jesus had done. When Christians suffered, they were enabled to enter more fully into the experience of their Lord.

Peter's language in verses 13-14 carried other vivid details which are noteworthy. The term translated "share" (v. 13) came from a more familiar Greek word, koinōneō, which conveyed the idea of partnership. When Christians suffer for their faith, Christ is their partner in pain.

Again, the "if" clause which introduced verse 14 is grammatically a first class conditional declaration. This construction assumes that what is stated was, or would become, actual fact. Thus, Peter wrote: If you are reproached for the name of Christ— and you are, or you will be . . .!

Also note that the word "blessed" (v. 14) is the same Greek word which Jesus used to introduce each of the Beatitudes in the Sermon on the Mount (Matt. 5:3-11).

Furthermore, the Greek word doxēs, or "glory," appeared in 1 Peter 4:13 and 4:14. In verse 13, the reference was to the glory of Christ which is to be revealed sometime in the future. This likely was another reference to Peter's expectation of Christ's imminent return. In verse 14, however, the reference is to a glory which is present. "The spirit of glory and of God" rests on Christians as they are undergoing persecution and trial.

The idea reflected Old Testament thought patterns. As the glory (or presence) of God rested on Mount Sinai, the tabernacle, or the Temple, so the glory or presence of God would rest on Christians in times of duress.

Avoiding Evil (4:15)

Having pointed clearly to the blessedness of Christians who suffer in Christ's name, Peter quickly asserted that a Christian should not suffer some things. He wrote: "But let none of you suffer as a murderer, or a thief, or a wrongdoer, or a mischief-maker" (v. 15).

Four specific categories of moral evil are mentioned in verse 15. The first two crimes of murder and theft should be understood clearly. The third offense was a kind of umbrella term for any kind of evil behavior. Earlier in his letter, Peter had used this same word on two occasions (2:12,14).

Peter's fourth area of concern in verse 15 was more unusual. In fact, the word translated "mischief-maker" is found only in this reference in the New Testament. Some interpreters thought that Peter might have coined this Greek word. Literally, it meant "an overseer of what belongs to other people." The word has been translated: "a busybody" (KJV); "a meddler in other men's matters" (ASV); "a spy" (Phillips).

Rather than high-handed espionage, "mischief-maker" probably referred to the temptation to be overly "nosey" about other people's affairs. Christians were to be caring persons, but they were not to make a nuisance of themselves, meddling in matters which were not their legitimate concern.

Glorifying God as a Christian (4:16)

The last verse in the section 4:12-16 is of special interest because it includes one of the three uses of the name "Christian" in the New Testament. (See Acts 11:26; 26:28.) Peter wrote: "Yet if one suffers as a Christian, let him not be ashamed, but under that name let him glorify God" (v. 16). This statement may have been a bit autobiographical for Peter. Once he had been ashamed to identify with Christ's name and suffer whatever consequences might come (Mark 14:66-71). Now, he was not ashamed; and he encouraged his friends in the provinces to take their stand with him "under that name."

The End Means Judgment (4:17-19)

Where Judgment Begins (4:17)
Before Peter closed the passage 4:12-19, he sounded one more note about the eschaton's nature. As much as human nature may recoil from the idea, Peter declared in no uncertain terms that the end will mean judgment: "For the time has come for judgment to begin with the household of God; and if it begins with us, what will be the end of those who do not obey the gospel of God" (v. 17)?

The Greek language had two words for **time**—chronos and kairos. **Chronos** referred primarily to the simple measuring or spacing of time, and the recounting of the duration of time. Chronos obviously gave us several English words like chronology, chronic, chronicle, chronometer. In contrast to this, **kairos** referred to a time or times which were unusually opportune, seasonable, and filled with significant meaning.

When Peter wrote the statement, "The time has come," he used the Greek word kairos. He was not referring just to the passing of another day or period of time. He was writing of a most pivotal season whose time had come. Peter believed that Christ's return was imminent, and he evidently saw the suffering which Christians would undergo as a part of God's judgment. God had some part in this smelting process, as Christians were made to pass through times of fiery ordeal in order that the quality of their faith might be tested and proved. When Peter wrote that this judgment would begin with "the household of God," he had the Christian believers as a whole in mind. This phrase also can be translated: the family of God. The words described what we today would call the congregation or the church.

The phrase "if it begins with us" is another first-class conditional sentence in Greek construction. The grammar meant that Peter was convinced judgment would begin with the people who had been closest to God, that is, believers in Christ. In Peter's mind, this question was not debatable.

And What of the Ungodly (4:18)?

Peter's conviction, however, created something of a dilemma for him. If God's judgment comes on Christian people first, what will happen to those persons who never have made the faintest attempt to obey the gospel? At this point, Peter quoted one of the Proverbs which seemed to say exactly what he was thinking:

" *'If the righteous man is scarcely*
saved,
where will the impious and sinner
appear" (v. 18; Prov. 11:31)?

In this context, the word translated **impious** meant the ungodly or wicked persons. **Sinner** meant *the irreligious* individual or *one who had missed God's way, God's mark for living.*

Both Peter and the Proverbs' writer's emphasis was human beings' absolute hopelessness without God. By pointing to the dark consequences of being without God in the world, Peter hoped to stir a greater loyalty among the Christians who were on the verge of suffering an in-depth purge.

Living in Trust (4:19)

Against the backdrop of possible ultimate hopelessness, Peter wrote one of his greatest affirmations of assurance and trust: "Therefore let those who suffer according to God's will do right and entrust their souls to a faithful Creator" (v. 19).

Peter believed that the end of all things was immediately at hand. He thought that the Christians were facing a time of intense harassment and persecution. Again he was urging the believers to make sure that when they did suffer, they were suffering according to God's will. Peter echoed what he had expressed earlier (v. 15; also 2:20). He appealed to his friends to suffer only for doing right, not for doing wrong. Peter's clinching statement was that they all, in the last analysis, had to "entrust their souls to a faithful Creator." From an academic point of view, this line is interesting because only in this verse and in Romans 1:25 is God referred to specifically in the New Testament as "Creator." The most stirring truth in this line, however, is the picture which lies behind the word translated **entrust.** This verb was an old word, a kind of bank figure which meant *to deposit.* No banks existed in Peter's day, as we know banks today. The word technically referred to depositing money with a trusted friend. With no banks and really few safe places to deposit money, a person going on a long trip often would leave his money in the safekeeping of a reliable friend. The friend was honor bound to keep the deposit safely intact.

Peter used the analogy of leaving money with a friend to assure his friends in the provinces that they confidently could entrust their lives to God's safekeeping. He would be absolutely dependable. Jesus used this same word when he spoke from the cross saying, " 'Father, into thy hands I *commit* my spirit' " (Luke 23:46).

Lessons for Life from 1 Peter 4:7-19

The Christian faith affirms that time and this world order as we know it someday will end.—To be sure, the imminent end of things which Peter expected has not occurred. Across the centuries, many individuals and/or groups have set the date for the *eschaton.* One of the most recent dates was set for June 28, 1981, by a Christian group in Arizona. Although these groups arise from different backgrounds, they all share one thing in common: To date, all have been wrong. Basically, Jesus said three things about his second coming and the end of time: (1) " 'I will come again' " (John 14:3). (2) " 'Of that day and hour no one knows, not even the angels of heaven, nor the Son, but the Father only' " (Matt. 24:36). (3) " 'Therefore you also must be ready; for the Son of man is coming at an hour you do not expect' " (Matt. 24:44). Of these three statements from Jesus, we may be certain. However, our main concern should not be timing but whether or not we are ready.

Expecting Christ's imminent return did not cause the first-century Christians to have an ethic of withdrawal or escape.—They remained in the mainstream of life and demonstrated their faith in action by loving one another, practicing hospitality, and doing various ministries.

With confidence, Christians may entrust their lives and destinies to a faithful Creator. God is absolutely dependable; he will keep that which we have entrusted to him. We never need to fear that he will fail or forsake us.

---

1. "God, I want to Live!" *Time,* June 2, 1980, pp. 26-31.
2. Elmer G. Hormighausen, *The Interpreter's Bible* (Nashville: Abingdon Press, 1957), 12:139.
3. A. T. Robertson, *Word Pictures in the New Testament* (Nashville: Broadman Press, 1933), 6:125.
4. William Barclay, *The Letters of James and Peter* (Philadelphia: The Westminster Press, 1976), 6:301.

120

Personal Learning Activities

1. Peter expected the end of all things to occur after a lengthy delay. True_____ False_____
2. When Peter wrote that "love covers a multitude of sins," he probably meant that love _____ many wrongs. (Select the proper response from the list.)
   (1) Overlooks   (3) Forgives
   (2) Hides   (4) Makes up for
3. Peter indicated that only a select, privileged few have *charisma*. True_____ False_____
4. Peter grouped God's gifts to people in two major divisions. From the list, choose the correct divisions.
   ____(1) Leadership   ____(3) Rendering service
   ____(2) Speaking for God ____(4) Magnetic personality
5. Peter listed four areas of evil that Christians should avoid. From the list, select the proper response.
   ____(1) Lying   ____(4) Stealing
   ____(2) Cheating   ____(5) Doing wrong
   ____(3) Murdering   ____(6) Meddling

Answers:
1. False; 2. (3); 3. False; 4. (2) (3); 5. (3), (4), (5), (6).

9

Life in the Church: Mirror of Our Faith
1 Peter 5:1-5

> The church does not exist in order to conquer its foes; God does that for it. On the contrary, it exists in order to pour out its life in service—healing the sick, casting out demons, cleansing lepers, restoring sight for the blind, providing food for the hungry, giving rest to the weary, making homes for the homeless, bringing comfort to the distraught, preaching peace to those near and far. Like Jesus himself, it lives by dying, pouring out its life to satisfy human need wherever and in whatever form it finds it.[1]

During my college years, I served as a BSU summer missionary to Hawaii. Our mission group was made up of thirteen students from nine states. I was assigned to work with churches in the city of Honolulu, on the island of Oahu.

Well-known landmarks like Pearl Harbor, Diamond Head, Waikiki Beach, and Nuuana Pali became familiar sites to us that summer. But we also learned firsthand of our Baptist churches' ministry in Hawaii—Olivet, Wahiawa, Waialae, Nuuana. As summer missionaries, our primary assignment was to help in Vacation Bible Schools and youth revivals. Needless to say, we had many unforgettable experiences that summer.

For example, one evening after a youth revival service in the University Baptist Church in Honolulu, a group of college-age young people were sharing an impromptu time of fellowship and serious discussion. During that summer, the University Church still was meeting in a building which once had been a large residence. The youth group had gravitated to the kitchen to have some cokes and pretzels.

Mostly, however, the group wanted to talk about the Christian faith. A young man named Seiji, who was a junior student at the University of Hawaii, had visited in the revival service that evening. He was a friend of some of the Oriental young people in the church, but he was not a Christian.

Like many of his peers had found, I discovered that Seiji had a discerning mind. His questions about the Christian faith were deep and probing. Rather than asking about surface matters, Seiji was concerned about the virgin birth of Christ, the idea of the Trinity, and the possibility of the resurrection. His questions about eternal destiny were extremely personal.

"My grandparents," he said, "lived in a remote mountain village in Japan where to my knowledge, the story of Jesus never had been told. They died as Buddhists without hearing of Christ. What does your faith say about them?"

As fledgling college theologians, we wrestled that evening with some of the great doctrines of our faith. The spirit of openness, searching, and genuine commitment was refreshing. Some of the young people in the group had become Christians from Buddhist backgrounds. They warmly shared their Christian testimonies. Our discussion seemed to produce some answers, but other areas remained somewhat beyond our grasp.

The hour became late, and we had to go. As Seiji was leaving, he spoke this parting word at the door: "You haven't answered all of my questions tonight, but I'll be back. You Christians have something which I don't have, and I am determined to know what it is!"

Seiji's words that evening were a clear affirmation of something I believe even more strongly today: A loving, committed, demonstrated life of intelligent faith through the church is one of the most convincing Christian witnesses we can give to the unbelieving world. Incidentally, that fall when I was back on my college campus, a letter came to me reporting that Seiji had made his profession of faith in Christ and had joined the baptismal class at the University Church in Honolulu.

As we read 1 Peter 5, we find that the author declared his strong conviction: Life in the church should mirror our faith in Jesus Christ. Peter's first-century counsel in this regard continues to speak clearly to us as twentieth-century church members. How we conduct ourselves in our churches is crucial.

Counsel for Church Leaders (5:1-4)

Peter had admonished his friends to entrust their lives to the safe-keeping of a faithful Creator-God. Now he turned to write something about the quality of life which Christians should reflect within the church. His opening exhortation addressed the leaders of the first-century churches.

Appeal to Elders (5:1)

The word of strong personal appeal which Peter had used earlier (2:11) appears again: "So I exhort the elders among you, as a fellow elder and a witness of the sufferings of Christ as well as a partaker in the glory that is to be revealed" (v. 1).

Who were the **elders**—the *presbuterous*? As this paragraph develops, the elders obviously were leaders in the churches. Basically, the Greek word in verse 1 meant exactly what the English translation implies—an older person. In the early church, however, this word came to refer to some of the appointed or official leaders within the churches.

Initially, the word was used in the New Testament in connection with Paul's first missionary journey. As Paul and Barnabas began their return to Jerusalem, retracing their steps across Asia Minor, they "appointed elders . . . in every church" in the towns and cities where they had been (Acts 14:23, my italics). As Paul was en route back to Jerusalem from the third missionary journey, he summoned "the elders of the church" at Ephesus to meet him in Miletus for a fond farewell (Acts 20:17, my italics).

Other uses of the word *elder* are found in Paul's letters which we know as the Pastoral Epistles. For example, he wrote: "Let the elders who rule well be considered worthy of double honor, especially those who labor in preaching and teaching" (1 Tim. 5:17). Or, again, in writing to Titus, Paul declared: "This is why I left you in Crete, that you might amend what was defective, and appoint elders in every town as I directed you" (Titus 1:5).

The various references indicate that in Christian usage, the word *elder* came to be employed as a title for pastoral leaders in the churches. The title seemed to relate primarily to the respect in which the pastor was held.[2]

Another title, **bishop**, was used to describe the functional service of pastors (1 Tim. 3:1-7). The word **bishop**, *episkopos*, meant overseer. In one reference, Paul apparently used these words in close proximity to refer to the same office or person within the church (Titus 1:5,7). We conclude, then, that the elders whom Peter addressed in his letter were the pastor-teachers in the churches in provinces of Asia Minor.

Like the peroration of an earnest legal defense, Peter was preparing his final exhortation for the elders in the churches whom he had addressed in his letter. He mentioned three personal qualifications which formed the basis of his appeal.

First, Peter identified himself as a "fellow elder." In his salutation, Peter described himself as "an apostle" (1:1). However in 5:1, he had no desire to pull any rank or to get hung-up in matters of protocol. His phrase "fellow elder"—which occurs only in this verse in the New Testament—reflected a degree of modesty and humility on Peter's part. Rather than to imply in the slightest way that he was above the church leaders, Peter openly declared that he was one of them and one with them.

Peter also wrote that he was "a witness of the sufferings of Christ." The Greek word **witness** meant *eyewitness*. Peter not only had suffered as a witness for his faith, he had witnessed Jesus' actual suffering in the Lord's Passion. Peter's words about Jesus, and his appeal for loyalty under fire, had the ring of authenticity.

Peter declared that he was a "partaker in the glory that is to be revealed." The word translated **partaker** is a form of the Greek word *koinōnia*. It meant *one who was a partner* or *one who shared*. The phrase about the glory to be revealed may refer to Peter's anticipation of the end of time and to Jesus' return. More likely, it referred to Peter's experience of being with Jesus at the time of the transfiguration (Mark 9:2-8). Along with James and John, Peter momentarily saw the Lord's glory in Jesus' face. Peter's language is similar to his reference to Jesus' transfiguration in his second letter (2 Pet. 1:17-18).

Charge to Tend God's Flock (5:2-3)

Having reestablished his credentials, Peter spelled out his appeal to the elders. "Tend the flock of God that is your charge, not by constraint but willingly, not for shameful gain but eagerly, not as domineering over those in your charge but being examples to the flock" (vv. 2-3).

The urgency of Peter's exhortation is marked by the imperative verb form which he used to introduce this sentence. He wrote: "Tend the flock." In the Greek language both words **tend** and

flock came from the same root stem, *poimēn,* which meant *shepherd.* In the original language, Peter used alliteration: *poimanate to en humin poimnion.*

The word translated "tend" is the same word which Jesus spoke to Peter on the shore of the Sea of Galilee when he said, "Tend my sheep" (John 21:16). Evidently, Peter had taken Jesus' counsel to heart; now he passed it almost verbatim to other persons who would be responsible for the care and nurture of new Christians.

The imagery of the words "tend" and "flock" pointed to the general task of shepherding. Often the figure of the shepherd caring for his sheep was used in the Old Testament to describe God's relationship to Israel (Isa. 40:11; Ps. 23). Jesus also used this metaphor. He called himself "the good shepherd," and he spoke of laying down his life for the sheep (John 10:11,14,17-18).

No analogy is more all-encompassing than that of tending a flock to picture the relationships which should be fostered within the family of God in the church. "To **tend** means to nourish with a proper diet, to protect with vigilant watchfulness, to heal from the bramble hurt, and to strengthen for the possible assault. Tending refers to the whole vast range of service which God requires for the spiritual maturing of his people."[3] This is the kind of ministry which Peter urged the elders to give their respective churches.

In the Greek text, the phrase "that is your charge" is literally: *among you.* The phrase referred to the fact that the churches had many elders, each one having his part of God's flock. His primary responsibility was to serve that group. The phrase "your charge" appears in the next verse.

Peter added three further qualifying phrases to describe the ministry which he was urging the elders to provide for the people in the churches. He did this by contrasting negative and positive ways of doing Christian ministries:

Negative	Positive
not by constraint	but willingly
not for shameful gain	but eagerly
not as domineering	but being examples

The phrase **not by constraint** meant that *the elder was not to do his pastoral ministry out of a sense of compulsion.* His attitude should not reflect a spirit which seemed to say: I'm doing this for you only because I have to! Instead, his attitude about his total ministry should reflect a willing spirit.

The phrase **not for shameful gain** meant that *the elder was not* to become a person greedy for material profit. His attitude should not reflect a spirit which seemed to say: I'm doing this for you only because I'm getting paid, and I really deserve more than you are willing to pay! Instead, the elder should do his ministry eagerly with an enthusiasm which would say: I'm going to serve you to the extent of my ability and your need. I am willing to live within the material guidelines which have been set for my office.

Probably, the elders were paid some prescribed stipend. Peter was not condemning a reasonable or generous remuneration to the elders. He was condemning the shameful, sordid lust for money.

The phrase **not as domineering** meant that the elders were not to lord it over the people in the churches. This is the same Greek word which Jesus used to describe how the Gentiles exercised authority over one another (Mark 10:42). Jesus added: "But it shall not be so among you; but whoever would be great among you must be your servant" (Mark 10:43).

Positively stated, Peter's exhortation urged the elders to be "examples to the flock" (v. 3). An interesting distinction in shepherding should be made at this point between the ways that eastern and western shepherds go about their work. In the west, the shepherd always is at the back of the flock, driving the sheep. In the eastern culture from which Peter was writing, the shepherd walked in front of the sheep, leading them in the way. Peter wanted the elders to be exemplary leaders, but he did not want them to drive the people.

Reminder of Reward (5:4)
Peter closed his counsel to the elders by reminding them of whose service they were in and what reward they might anticipate receiving: "And when the chief Shepherd is manifested you will obtain the unfading crown of glory" (v. 4).

Israel's faith in the Shepherd's care was given graphic expression in the matchless words of Psalm 23. Again, in the face of the priests' bogus shepherding behavior, Jesus declared himself to be the Good Shepherd who would lay down his life for the sheep (John 10:11,14-15). The author of the Letter to the Hebrews called Jesus "the great shepherd of the sheep" (Heb. 13:20). But only Peter designated Jesus as being "the chief Shepherd" (1 Pet. 5:4).

You may have been in a work situation in which the supervising person affectionately was called "The Chief." In a real sense, Peter was saying that the elders were undershepherds, serving under the Lord's supervision.

The word "manifested" in verse 4 almost certainly refers to Peter's expectancy of Jesus' imminent return. This is one of the terms which often was used to refer to Christ's second coming. Peter envisioned this decisive event as being a time of reward for those who had been faithful in their Christian service.

Peter described the expected reward as "the unfading crown of glory." The unfading nature of this Christian crown was to be contrasted with the perishable nature of crowns which were given to victorious soldiers and athletes. These crowns—made from flowers, ivy, and sometimes vegetables—withered quickly. The Christian crown would be forever.

The Greek language had two different words for crown—*diadēma* and *stephanos*. The *diadēma* crown, as a rule, was a sign of royalty. A person received the right to wear this crown primarily because of his or her royal lineage. In a sense, we could say that the wearing of the *diadēma* was an accident of birth.

The *stephanos* crown, however, was a badge of honor which was worn as a prize for victory. It was conferred as a public salute for distinguished service in war or peace. Also, it was worn as a badge of office. The *stephanos* crown, if you please, was earned by merit. Peter used this word when he described the crown which faithful elders and Christians would receive at the Lord's return.

Counsel for Church Members (5:5)

Having addressed the elders with the first part of his final exhortation, Peter then appealed to the members at large: "Likewise you that are younger be subject to the elders. Clothe yourselves, all of you, with humility toward one another, for 'God opposes the proud, but gives grace to the humble' " (v. 5).

In verse 5, to note that the churches were sufficiently established to include more than one age group is interesting. Although at this time the majority of believers still would have been first-generation Christians, congregations included older Christians and younger Christians.

Peter appealed to the younger Christians to be good followers of "the elders." In this context, the reference is probably to age rather than to official church status. As in verse 1, "elders" could refer to pastors. More likely, this simply refers to older Christians whose honorable lives and faithful service deserved respect and emulation from Christians who were younger.

Peter did not want a divisive generation gap to develop in the congregations he addressed. Then and now, churches have needed a wholesome balance between the older, established generation and the newer, take-over generation. Churches need both the enthusiasm of youth and the seasoned wisdom of age.

Peter's next counsel was addressed to older and younger Christians—"all of you," he wrote. He urged the entire membership of the congregations to clothe themselves with humility.

The Greek word translated "clothe" appears only in verse 5 in the New Testament. The root stem of the verb was *kombos,* which meant knot. The verb form referred to a garment being tied over other garments. It especially was used to describe a frock or apron worn by slaves.

Likely, Peter was recalling Jesus' example in the footwashing experience in the upper room (John 13:1-14); therefore, Peter called on his Christian friends to demonstrate a genuine, selfless concern for one another.

Peter supported his counsel with a quotation from Proverbs: "God opposes the proud, but gives grace to the humble" (3:34, Septuagint). As was indicated at the beginning of this textbook chapter, like Jesus, the church lives by dying—by pouring out its life to satisfy human need.

Lessons for Life from 1 Peter 5:1-5

The early churches' pastors were involved in preaching and teaching.—In his letter, Peter used the word "elder" to refer to pastoral leaders. Paul sometimes used the word "bishop" to refer to pastoral leaders. These persons were to lead God's people in the churches by means of proclamation (kērugma) and instruction (didachē). We sometimes hear discussions as to whether the pastor's task is primarily a preaching or a teaching responsibility. The New Testament pattern in this regard was not either-or, but both-and. Matthew wrote that as Jesus began his ministry, "he went about all Galilee, teaching . . . and preaching" (Matt. 4:23). Today, good pastors have a wholesome balance of these functions.

The role of the shepherd remains the ideal model for what a pastor should be to his people.—In the Middle East, shepherds always go before their sheep to lead them in the way. This custom is reflected clearly in the Shepherd Psalm: "He leads me beside still waters.... He leads me in paths of righteousness for his name's sake" (Ps. 23:2-3). In contrast to this, western shepherds go behind their sheep, driving them along the way. Good pastoral leaders will follow the eastern, not the western, shepherding model. They will lead people rather than drive them.

The church should be a family of people who experience no sharp generation gap.—In a healthy congregation, both the young and the elderly will feel welcomed and needed. Rather than polarizing one another into opposing camps, the young and the elderly should complement one another.

---

1. E. Glenn Hinson, *The Church: Design for Survival* (Nashville: Broadman Press, 1967), p. 35.

2. Ray Summers, *The Broadman Bible Commentary* (Nashville: Broadman Press, 1972), 12:169.

3. Elmer G. Homrighausen, *The Interpreter's Bible* (New York: Abingdon Press, 1957), 12:150.

Personal Learning Activities

1. The elders whom Peter addressed in his letter probably were the deacons in the various congregations. True____ False____
2. According to Dr. McClanahan, by the phrase "the glory that is to be revealed" Peter probably meant _____. (Select the proper response from the list.)
   (1) Christ's return   (3) The transfiguration
   (2) Heaven   (4) The triumph of the church
3. Peter indicated some positive ways that the elders should minister. From the list, choose the correct ways.
   ____(1) Willingly   ____(3) Eagerly
   ____(2) By constraint   ____(4) By being examples
4. In 1 Peter 5:4, Peter used the title _____ to refer to Christ. (Select the proper answer from the list.)
   (1) King   (3) Shepherd
   (2) Lamb   (4) Lord
5. Peter admonished the younger Christians to _____ the elders. (Choose the correct answer from the list.)
   (1) Ignore   (3) Be subject to
   (2) Pity   (4) Support

Answers: 1. False; 2. (3); 3. (1), (3), (4); 4. (3); 5. (3).

10

Remember—We Serve a Triumphant Lord

1 Peter 5:6-14

But I shall go down from this airy space, this
*   swift, white, peace, this stinging exultation,*
And time will close about me, and my soul stir
*   to the rhythm of the daily round.*
Yet, having known, life will not press so close,
*   and always I shall feel time ravel thin about me;*
For once I stood
In the white windy presence of eternity.[1]

In my personal files, I have a letter from a young man which
reminds me of the last verses from 1 Peter 5. The letter is one of
those unusual, unforgettable pieces of correspondence which I
always will treasure. It is a long letter—five hand-written pages.
The young man wrote from a motel room where he was staying
overnight while he traveled his sales route. I would not have
known of the dramatic, personal episode which he recounted had
he not written his letter. This is the story which he told.

Two weeks prior to his writing the letter, the young man sat in
an opening Sunday morning revival service where I was the guest
preacher. Unknown to me, this young man's life was tottering on
the brink of moral collapse. He and his wife were estranged. The
efforts at reconciliation which the pastor of the church had made
were beginning to break down. The young man's wife had been an
inactive member of the church where we were that morning in the
capital city of their state. He had only a nominal Christian background.

131

In the counseling that the couple had received from the pastor, the young man felt that his wife had not been totally honest in what she had shared. What he believed to be her deception in this area frustrated and angered him. He had started drinking again—heavily—away from home.

In fact, at a local tavern in his city just that previous week, he had met a "go-go" dancer with whom he talked for several hours. They had planned a rendezvous-date for the Sunday afternoon that the revival began—her only day off from work. As he put it, "It was like I was walking a tightrope during the church service that Sunday morning. Before the day was to end, I was contemplating letting the last grain of self-respect I had go down the drain."

During the worship service, the young man was moved profoundly by part of the sermon. He was so moved that he left the service, as he expressed it, "weeping so hard that I could hardly see." Incidentally, the specific comments in the sermon which had touched the man so deeply were not a part of my manuscript outline. This experience is a strong affirmation to me that the Holy Spirit does invade the dynamic setting of preaching.

Although both the husband and the wife were in the service that day, due to their estrangement they were not sitting together. In fact, they had come to church that morning in different cars. When the young man arrived at home, his wife could tell that he had been crying. He shared with her some of the things that he had felt in his morning worship experience. He told her of his plan to meet the "go-go" dancer that afternoon, but indicated that this rendezvous never would take place. He confessed his sense of guilt about even thinking of cheating on his wife in this way.

The depth of his repentance brought the wife to tears. She confessed to her faults which were keeping the marriage from being reconciled. They affirmed to one another their desire to be persons worthy of love, trust, and confidence.

The revival closed on Friday evening, and I flew home on Saturday. I knew nothing of what I have just written. On the following Sunday morning, however, the couple made significant public decisions in their church. The young man professed his faith in Christ, and his wife reaffirmed her faith and dedicated her life anew to genuine Christian living.

The young man closed his letter: "My mind and heart are wide open. I've joined a Sunday School class, and will start in Church

Training next week. I'm in a motel room just now 130 miles from home, but I'm no longer alone. I hope and pray never to turn my back on my Savior again."

The young man and his wife learned that neither as a couple nor as individuals could they succeed in life by going their own ways. Head-strong and selfish, they came close to losing some of the most precious gifts that God can give. When they came to Christ and his church, however, life for them suddenly was mended, renewed, and stabilized.

See if the personal incident that I have related does not remind you of Peter's closing words of encouragement to the young Christians in Asia Minor. Peter's final paragraph is permeated by an imperative sense of urgency. In fact, I find that Peter called on his friends to demonstrate four affirmative attitudes as their lives became increasingly difficult. They were to be humble, trustful, vigilant, and confident.

Be Humble (5:6)

Peter began his closing paragraph by echoing the humility theme which he had sounded immediately before verse 6 with a quotation from the Old Testament: " 'God opposes the proud, but gives grace to the humble' " (5:5; see Prov. 3:34). Peter now wrote: "Humble yourselves therefore under the mighty hand of God, that in due time he may exalt you" (v. 6).

In the Greek language, the sentence in verse 6 opens with an imperative verb form. Thus, Peter's words were a strong exhortation. We could convey his mood best by punctuating the sentence with an exclamation mark. Here, Peter donned the role of a preacher of humility. A great English poet later wrote that humility was "the highest virtue, mother of them all."[2] Peter viewed humility in the same way.

Real humility is not a sense of self-depreciation which makes a person feel worthless. Rather, genuine humility is a sense of lowliness which results from a vision of life's grandeur and greatness. Instead of trying to play the role of Creator, humble persons are aware of their creatureliness. They have a growing appreciation for what they have received from God and from other significant people in their lives.

Peter called on his friends to humble themselves "under the

mighty hand of God" (v. 6). People of that day increasingly were learning what it meant to bow down to mighty Rome. For centuries, the mailed fist had been a sign of oppression. Ordinarily, people who humbled themselves under such martial power were ground further and further into the dust.

Peter declared that harsh subjection would not be the case for those who humbled themselves under God's hand. Peter wrote that rather than driving people into a further state of depression and loss of identity, God would exalt those who humbly related to him in faith and love.

As long as the young man and his wife who were mentioned earlier in this chapter stubbornly tried to make their way by giving no allegiance to God, their lives and their marriage rapidly deteriorated. When they humbly confessed their sins to one another and to God, almost immediately a process of reconciliation and uplifting began for them.

Be Trustful (5:7)

Peter continued to offer encouragement. He wrote: "Cast all your anxieties on him, for he cares about you" (v. 7). The Greek word for **cast** appears only here and in Luke 19:35 in the New Testament. It meant to throw on, as the disciples threw their garments on the colt on which Jesus rode as he made his royal entry into Jerusalem (Luke 19:35). Peter's words in verse 7 recall a line from one of the psalms: "Cast your burden on the Lord, and he will sustain you" (Ps. 55:22).

The Revised Standard Version's translation of this verse is a good translation of the Greek text. Two different Greek words were used to indicate people's burdens and God's care. The first word is translated best as "anxieties" (RSV). Jesus used a verb form of this same word three times in the Sermon on the Mount with the meaning, "Do not be anxious" (Matt. 6:25,31,34). The second word (melei) was an impersonal verb which meant there is a care, it concerns.

Peter indicated to his readers that not only does God have a mighty hand, but he also has broad shoulders and a strong back. We can throw our anxieties on him. Far more than some unmoved mover or distant deity, God is a caring, concerned Heavenly Father for all who will receive his love.

Be Vigilant (5:8-9)

Peter became more impassioned in the third dimension of his closing counsel to the believers in Asia Minor, if that were possible. "Be sober, be watchful," he wrote. "Your adversary the devil prowls around like a roaring lion, seeking some one to devour. Resist him, firm in your faith, knowing that the same experience of suffering is required of your brotherhood throughout the world" (vv. 8-9).

Be Alert (5:8)

Again, Peter used imperative verb forms to begin his exhortation. Exclamation marks would be the proper punctuation after "Be sober! Be watchful!" Twice before, Peter had used the word "sober" in his appeal to his friends (1:13; 4:7). Now for a third time, he urged them to have this mental attitude. As previously indicated, although the word could refer to abstaining from the use of alcoholic beverages (1 Thess. 5:6-8), this was not Peter's primary concern. He was urging his friends to remain calm; they were not to lose their cool. Rather than referring to drinking habits as such, he was calling on them to keep a poised, razor-sharp mind-set.

The Greek word translated **watchful** meant *to be awake in contrast to being asleep.* With its imperative form, we could say that the meaning in verse 8 was *to be wide awake.* Peter was appealing for a kind of alertness among the believers which made a good sentry. Put these two words together and Peter was urging, "Be vigilant!"

Beware of the Adversary (5:8)

The reason Peter called for such vigilance was because he rightly saw that Christians are engaged in a spiritual warfare. We have an **adversary** (v. 8), an accuser. In the original language, this word was an old legal term which technically referred to *an opponent in a lawsuit.* In popular usage of the first century, the word had come to mean *an enemy.*

Peter's usage, however, was more explicit. He was referring to *the* enemy, the devil. In the Greek, the word **devil** literally meant *slanderer.*

Peter's simile to describe the devil was graphic. He pictured the devil to be like a roaring lion prowling around, seeking to devour someone. His imagery may have been borrowed from Psalm 22:13. If you have been visiting in a zoo at feeding time, you likely have heard the roar of lions. A lion roars to express his hunger. Thus Peter described the devil as being like a roaring lion, gripped by the rage of hunger, prowling the earth seeking to devour someone.

C. S. Lewis, one of the great British apologists (defenders) for the Christian faith in this century, has written that modern men and women tend to make two equally incorrect errors in addressing the matter of the devil: "There are two equal and opposite errors into which our race can fall about the devils. One is to disbelieve in their existence. The other is to believe, and to feel an excessive and unhealthy interest in them. They themselves are equally pleased by both errors and hail a materialist or a magician with the same delight."[3]

Peter avoided both of the pitfalls in his understanding of the spiritual warfare in which Christians are involved. In his letter, he reflected neither a denial of the devil nor an exaggerated fear of the devil's influence. But Peter took the devil seriously. He knew that an insidious, debilitating, clever power was at work continually in the world trying to destroy all of God's work for good. He knew that the devil's purpose was to ruin men and women. Peter saw that eternal vigilance was the price of freedom for God's children.

Resist the Devil (5:9)

Therefore, Peter urged his friends to stand up against the lethal influence which would try to demolish them. Using another imperative verb form, Peter wrote: "Resist him" (v. 9). The Greek word here literally meant *to stand against*. Peter knew that rolling over and playing dead was not sufficient opposition to put the devil to flight. Such cowardice never wins against the devil. Only a courage which takes a positive, aggressive stand will be able to "quench all the flaming darts of the evil one" (Eph. 6:16).

Peter saw the cure for overcoming the devil's tempting power to be a solid faith in God. The word translated **firm** in verse 9 was an old adjective in the Greek which meant *solid like a foundation*. Such an active faith is still the anchor which will hold when the strong winds blow.

Peter also reminded his friends in Asia Minor that they were not alone in experiencing grave conflict and suffering because of their Christian faith. The devil's influence was felt throughout the

world. Consequently, temptation, persecution, and suffering became the common lot of believers everywhere.

Be Confident (5:10-11)

We should note carefully that although Peter affirmed the reality of the ongoing spiritual warfare which Christians must endure,
he was confident that the ultimate victory would belong to God
and to God's people. With his expectancy of Christ's imminent
return, Peter thought that he and his peers already were living in
the fourth quarter of the game of life. They expected the final
whistle to be blown at any time. In those days, the blocking and
tackling on the playing field was fierce. However, the final outcome of the game already was decided. The devil and the forces of
evil had lost. God and the powers of righteousness had won.

Peter closed the body of his letter with a strong statement of
hope and confidence: "And after you have suffered a little while,
the God of all grace, who has called you to his eternal glory in
Christ, will himself restore, establish, and strengthen you. To him
be the dominion for ever and ever. Amen" (vv. 10-11).

Peter reflected an assurance which is found throughout the New
Testament. He believed that earnest skirmishes would continue to
be fought between good and evil. However, the decisive battle in
this conflict already had been fought and won. Jesus Christ had
lived, had died a real death on the cross, but had experienced a
real resurrection from the grave. The God of all grace had called
Christians to an eternal, everlasting glory in and through Christ.
This glory was a secure and unshakable inheritance. Peter used
three, perhaps four, key Greek words to affirm his confident faith
in this sure inheritance.

The first of Peter's key words is translated **restore.** Through
suffering, God would restore the believers. The Greek word com-
monly was used for setting a fractured bone. Also, it was used to
describe the mending of fishing nets (Mark 1:19). The word meant
to supply what was missing or to mend that which was broken.
"So suffering," wrote William Barclay, "if it is accepted in humility and trust and love, can add to a man's character that which is
lacking; it can repair the weaknesses, and add the greatness which
so far is not there."[4]

The second key word is translated **establish.** Through suffering,

137

God would establish the believers. The Greek word used in verse 10 meant *to make as solid as granite*. This is the same word which Luke used to describe how Jesus "*set his face*," determined to go to Jerusalem (Luke 9:41, my italics). God's promise is that individual believers' fragile weaknesses can pass through the forge of suffering and be transformed into a kind of strength which resembles a solid stone wall.

The third key word in verse 10 is translated **strengthen**. Through suffering, God would strengthen the believers. The Greek word here meant *to fill with strength* or *to make strong*. Suffering believers are never flabby Christians. Times of testing and affliction burn out the fatty tissue of our lives and boil us down to firm sinew and nerve.

Some ancient manuscripts include a further key word in verse 10. Whereas the Revised Standard Version omits the fourth word, the King James Version includes it. (However, read the footnote in the RSV.) The Greek word is translated **settle**. It meant *to lay the foundation*. Suffering and sorrow drive us to the bedrock of our faith. Life's trials can force us to push away the shifting sands of time in order to discover the One who is the solid rock. This rock is Jesus, the only One. On him, in the twentieth century as in the first century, believers may discover an adequate footing on which to stand.

The thought which Peter expressed in the key words was like a rising crescendo. The in-depth thrill of knowing what God in Christ would do for believers in trouble caused him to burst forth with a concluding doxology: "To him be the dominion for ever and ever. Amen" (v. 11).

Concluding Postscript (5:12-14)

The final words in 1 Peter are like a concluding postscript: "By Silvanus, a faithful brother as I regard him, I have written briefly to you, exhorting and declaring that this is the true grace of God; stand fast in it. She who is at Babylon, who is likewise chosen, sends you greetings; and so does my son Mark. Greet one another with the kiss of love. Peace to all of you that are in Christ" (vv. 12-14).

As Paul often did (Gal. 6:11-18; 2 Thess. 3:17-18), Peter likely wrote the concluding words in his own handwriting. They indicate that he was in the company of Silvanus, or Silas, and John Mark. Silvanus (v. 12) was the amanuensis, or secretary, who wrote most of the letter while Peter spoke. Probably, he was also the bearer of the letter to the churches in Asia Minor.

The reference to "Babylon" (v. 13) indicated that Peter likely was writing from Rome, as the mystical Babylon in Revelation was also the city of Rome. The kiss of love (v. 14) was a kiss on the cheek or forehead. Peter closed his letter with a benediction which echoed what he had written in the salutation—an earnest entry for peace.

Lessons for Life from 1 Peter 5:6-14

Christian humility is not a sense of self-depreciation which makes a person feel worthless, but a sense of lowliness which results from a vision of life's grandeur and greatness.—Rather than to feel continually that they are masters of their own fates and captains of their own souls, humble people have a growing appreciation for what they have received from God and from all other significant people in their lives. To humble oneself before God brings elevation, not subjugation.

The Christian faith takes the devil seriously.—As the arch adversary and accuser, the devil plays a crucial role in the parasitic realm of evil. Christians do not deny the devil, but neither do they give him an exaggerated role in human affairs. The devil's primary purpose is to ruin men and women. For God's children, eternal vigilance still is the price of freedom from the devil's influence.

The Christian faith rises to a crescendo of confident assurance that God and his people will endure and prevail.—Peter thought that he and his peers were living in the last days. They expected the final curtain to fall at any time. The battle between good and evil was fierce. The final outcome, however, was decided already. The devil and the forces of evil had lost. God and the powers of righteousness had won. The skirmishes between good and evil still go on. But our Christian confidence has not been shaken one whit. We still serve a triumphant Lord!

1. Eunice Tietjens, *Profiles from China* (New York: Alfred A. Knopf, Inc., 1917), p. 39. Used by permission.
2. Alfred Lord Tennyson, *Idylls of the King*, "The Holy Grail," lines 445-46.
3. C. S. Lewis, *The Screwtape Letters* (New York: The Macmillan Company, 1956), p. XXXI.
4. William Barclay, *The Letters of James and Peter* (Philadelphia: The Westminster Press, 1976), p. 324.

Personal Learning Activities

1. In Peter's thought, real humility was/is self depreciation. True____ False____

2. Peter stated that God would _____ those who humbly related to him in faith and love. (Choose the correct answer from the list.)
   (1) Discipline   (3) Exalt
   (2) Bless materially   (4) Protect

3. The word **devil** means *slanderer*. True____ False____

4. In popular usage in the first century, the term *devil* came to mean _____. (Choose the correct answer from the list.)
   (1) Enemy   (3) Lucifer
   (2) Demon   (4) Deceiver

5. Peter compared the devil to a _____. (Select the proper response from the list.)
   (1) Messenger of light   (3) Man
   (2) Lion   (4) Snake

6. Peter used striking words to affirm his faith in God's ability to ensure an eternal inheritance for Christians. From the list, select the terms.
   (1) Restore   (3) Strengthen
   (2) Establish   (4) Settle

Answers: 1. False; **2.** (3); **3.** True; **4.** (1); **5.** (2); **6.** (1), (2), (3), (4).

THE CHURCH STUDY COURSE

The Church Study Course consists of a variety of short-term credit courses for adults and youth and noncredit foundational units for children and preschoolers. The materials are for use in addition to the study and training curriculums made available to the churches on an ongoing basis.

Study courses and foundational units are organized into a system that is promoted by the Sunday School Board, 127 Ninth Avenue, North, Nashville, Tennessee 37234; by the Woman's Missionary Union, 600 North Twentieth Street, Birmingham, Alabama 35203; by the Brotherhood Commission, 1548 Poplar Avenue, Memphis, Tennessee 38104; and by the respective departments of the state conventions affiliated with the Southern Baptist Convention.

Study course materials are flexible enough to be adapted to the needs of any Baptist church. The resources are published in several different formats—textbooks of various sizes, workbooks, and kits. Each item contains a brief explanation of the Church Study Course and information on requesting credit. Additional information and interpretation are available from the participating agencies.

Types of Study and Credit

Adults and youth can earn study course credit through individual or group study. Teachers of courses or of foundational units are also eligible to receive credit.

1. Class Experience.—Group involvement with course material for the designated number of hours for the particular course. A person who is absent from one or more sessions must complete the "Personal Learning Activities" or other requirements for the course.
2. Individual Study.—This includes reading, viewing, or listening to course material and completing the specified requirements for the course.
3. Lesson Course Study.—Parallel use of designated study course material during the study of selected units in Church Program Organization periodical curriculum units. Guid-

ance for this means of credit appears in the selected periodical.

4. Institutional Study.—Parallel use of designated study course material during regular courses at educational institutions, including Seminary Extension Department courses. Guidance for this means of credit is provided by the teacher.

Credit is awarded for the successful completion of course of study. This credit is granted by the Church Study Course Awards Office, 127 Ninth Avenue, North, Nashville, Tennessee 37234, for the participating agencies. Form 151 (available free) is recommended for use in requesting credit.

When credit is issued to a person on request, the Awards Office sends two copies of a notice of credit earned to the church. The original copy of the credit slip should be filed by the study course clerk in the participant's record of training folder. The duplicate should be given to the person who earned the credit. Accumulated credits are applied toward leadership or member development diplomas, which are measures of learning, growth, development, and training.

Detailed information about the Church Study Course system of credits, diplomas, and record keeping is available from the participating agencies. Study course materials, supplementary teaching or learning aids, and forms for record keeping may be ordered from Baptist Book Stores.

The Church Study Course Curriculum
Credit is granted on those courses listed in the current copy of *Church Services and Materials Catalog* and *Baptist Book Store Catalog*. When selecting courses or foundational units, check the current catalogs to determine what study course materials are valid.

How to Request Credit for This Course
This book is the text for a course in the subject area Bible Study.

This course is designed for 5 hours of group study. Credit is awarded for satisfactory class experience with the study material for the minimum number of hours. A person who is absent from one or more sessions must complete the "Personal Learning Activities" or other requirements for the materials missed.

Credit also is allowed for use of this material in individual study and in institutional study, if so designated.

The following requirements must be met for credit in this course:

1. Read the book 1 *Peter: Message of Encouragement.*
2. Attend at least 5 hours of class study or complete all "Personal Learning Activities" (see end of each chapter). A class member who is absent from one or more class sessions must complete "Personal Learning Activities" on chapters missed. In such a case, the class member must turn in his or her paper by the date the teacher sets, usually within ten days following the last class.

Credit in this course may be earned through individual study. The requirements for such credit are:

1. Read the book.
2. Complete the "Personal Learning Activities."

Credit in this course may be earned through study in an educational institution, if so designated by a teacher. The requirements are:

1. Read the book.
2. Fulfill the requirements of the course taught at the institution.

After the course is completed, the teacher, the study course records librarian, the learner, or any person designated by the church should complete Form 151 ("Church Study Course Credit Request, Revised 1975") and send it to the Awards Office, 127 Ninth Avenue, North, Nashville, Tennessee 37234. In the back of this book the reader will find a form which may be cut out, filled in, and sent to the Awards Office.

CHURCH STUDY COURSE
ENROLLMENT/CREDIT REQUEST (FORM-725)

PERSONAL CSC NUMBER (If Known)

☐☐☐☐☐☐ — ☐☐☐ — 0 0 0

INSTRUCTIONS:

1. Please PRINT or TYPE.
2. COURSE CREDIT REQUEST—Requirements must be met. Use exact title.
3. ENROLLMENT IN DIPLOMA PLANS—Enter selected diploma title to enroll.
4. For additional information see the Church Study Course Catalog.
5. Duplicate additional forms as needed. Free forms are available from the Awards Office and State Conventions.

TYPE OF REQUEST: (Check all that apply)

☐ Course Credit
☐ Enrollment in Diploma Plan

☐ Address Change
☐ Name Change
☐ Church Change

☐ Mr.   ☐ Miss
☐ Mrs.

DATE OF BIRTH ⬆ | Month | Day | Year

REQUEST FOR

Name (First, Mi, Last)

Street, Route, or P.O. Box

City, State, Zip Code

CHURCH

Church Name

Mailing Address

City, State, Zip Code

COURSE CREDIT REQUEST

Use exact title

1.   1 Peter: Message of Encouragement

Use exact title

2.

Use exact title

3.

Use exact title

4.

Use exact title

5.

ENROLLMENT IN DIPLOMA PLANS

If you have not previously indicated a diploma(s) you wish to earn, or you are beginning work on a new one(s), select and enter the diploma title from the current Church Study Course Catalog. Select one that relates to your leadership responsibility or interest. When all requirements have been met, the diploma will be automatically mailed to your church. No charge will be made for enrollment or diplomas.

Title of diploma

1.

Age group or area ⬆

Title of diploma

2.

Age group or area

Signature of Pastor, Teacher, or Study Leader

Date

MAIL THIS
REQUEST TO

CHURCH STUDY COURSE AWARDS OFFICE
RESEARCH SERVICES DEPARTMENT
127 NINTH AVENUE, NORTH
NASHVILLE, TENNESSEE 37234

BSSB-725 (Rev. 9-81)